THE
R.I.P.

Mining the
Subconscious
Artifact

James Philip Beyor

PUBLICATIONS

This book was set in New Baskerville and was printed and bound in the United States of America.

9   8   7   6   5   4   3   2

Published by:	CT Publications P.O. Box 1070 Buchanan, VA 24066 Phone 540-254-1842 Fax 540-254-2870
Edited by:	M. Faizi
All illustrations by:	James Beyor
Cover design by:	Dunn & Associates
Typeset by:	Graffolio
Indexed by:	Writers Anonymous, Inc.
Printed by:	Rose Printing

Publication in Progress:
　　Beyor, James Philip.
　　　　The R.I.P.: mining the subconscious artifact / James Philip Beyor
　　　　p. cm.
　　　　Includes bibliographical references and index. Illustrated.
　　　　LCCN: 96-83419
　　　　ISBN 0-9651228-0-8

　　　　1. Philosophy. 2. Beyor, James Philip.   I. Title. II. Title: The RIP.
　　B945.B49R56 1996   191
　　　　　　　　　　　　　　　　　　　　　　　　　　QB196-20479

For Philip and Ada Beyor

The R.I.P.

Within all of us exists a First Voice.
Second Voice is an artifact composed of
Promise Extensions that are Agreed to be
the carriers of Duty.
However, original expression is found beneath words
in the Sensual Center:
Five Senses, perfect in every way.

The R.I.P.

in the Human Parallel of Consciousness,
leaves us to function with two severed halves:
To Be or Not To Be.
All that joins life to Self comes through Question,
for we think only when we Doubt;
for Thought is not Agreement but is Doubt Resolved.

The R.I.P.

is the severed Self
unhealed and guarded
for Reason Manifest.
Realize that Self is
the outgrowth of Awareness,
and Knowledge is product of
The Self in False Momentum;
trapped in Agreement,
afraid and alone in Blame.

Without R.I.P.

There is no Blame.

Without R.I.P.

The Human Creature is Complete.

CONTENTS

ILLUSTRATIONS

PREFACE

The R.I.P. was written for the thinker: One who, in aspiration to genuine Self-feeling has, by his dire will to the human being, a capacity for Self awareness and passive learning. The thinker is unafraid of question and he knows the sadness that comes with profound transitional feeling in a world made from Reason and Reason bias.

The thinker braves the difficulties of his own Self-awareness and struggles with asperity that stems from his reluctance to Agree with commonplace made truths. Through his Disagreement with accepted Virtue and through an ultimate quest for Self, the thinker comes to terms with original First Voice sensitivity. The thinker, through feeling, then, finds Impassionment. The thinker, then, through feeling, comes to know himself and all of humankind as the most gentle of all creatures on earth.

The human being is approaching a new Dark Age as he attempts to save and protect and control his symbolic marketplace—as he attempts to further progress, even when progress can no longer be furthered—and when the promise of Reason can no longer be fulfilled. In the name of progress, the Agreement process is becoming a last comportment of authority given to prescribe sickness or ineptness to anyone who will not Agree to sacred Word.

The R.I.P. in Parallel Consciousness is widening. The human creature is consumed by increasing and more perplexing Paradox. The Impasse of Reason paradox confines and restricts memory and enables reactionary beliefs to proliferate and thrive. The intractable seeds of fear are planted within the fertile ground that is the degenerative mind of the human being in reverse of original self and are used by consigned authority to hold and maintain position in Entity Trust that is Savior and the promise of Future Bright. The cost of future is the loss of will and the gain in future is enslavement. Human will is lost to a parasitic Entity that sucks The Creature of its Essence, its substance and its perspective for the cause of virtue and progress that can no longer produce value except as artifact.

What was once polished and gleaming through the virtue of Agreeable Hope is now ashen and faded. What was once subscription to value for Agreed value returned is now conscription of critical thought for applied and placated meaning of intention, no matter how empty is Intent and emotionally vacant. The Brotherhood of Impasse thrives on waste.

"Trust," we were told. "Have faith," we were told, and "Seek the truth," and "Do right." Who told us these things and with what authority?

Can we define right as anything other than rational knowledge of what is expected and what is opposed to what actually, through belief and intention, is right by submission?

Can truth be defined as anything other than Paradox based on belief for coordinated puppetry who hold office over Creature Fear? What is the Truth of Subconscious Implant, Symbolic Warrant and Perfect Blame Loop? We are trained in Truth by Agreement, and Truth is Hypocrisy. Perfect Hypocrisy is power offered in position and place and rank. It is the sitting upon the one side which is the only side—the one correct and true side—to rule the mono-dimensional world of The Word in Composmentis.

What is knowledge after the masks of Good, Right and Truth Failsafed are removed? What, then, is naked knowledge? Can there exist worth, value and a corresponding knowledge of truth that does not entail studied Blame with Reason feigned through Failed Agreement?

The Credited Good are vested with Word Empowerment and, through Provoker Function, positioned in rank with every legislated means of Authority and Authorized Momentum in the name of The Common Good.

Whether it is fact or fiction, existence reflects Subjection of The Will of Man through Belief. Truth is the destroyer of Civilized Man and his Knowledge Cabal is a knife through the human heart, through the human essence and through the very possibility of life itself.

Word from the Publisher

All people are born with insight. Some do not have use for it because they are pampered. Some people have need but are afraid to use it. Some people trade insight for job advantage. Most deliberately select not to use it because it is an encumbrance and it is self imposing.

The R.I.P. is exacting and explicit in its call to insight and in its deep concern for life and for the troubles to which the human being succumbs.

The R.I.P. cuts through foible and pretense and defines and affirms a very special First Voice: the First Voice that Mr. Beyor describes in detail. First Voice refuses the indignity of compromise. First Voice is our voice of excellence and it is a voice that is inherent within us all, available to serve the one gentle creature that is man and woman.

Marsha Faizi

I

I

THE R.I.P.

Reciprocity in Paradox

For now we see through a glass,
darkly but then face to face: now I
know in part; but then I shall know
even as also I am known.

—I Corinthians 13:1

THROUGH DEDUCTIVE THOUGHT, we may find much brighter
elements in the mind than mere terminology thrown into the
dross of our usual circumscribed factory think processing. By
subtraction of such ready-made and archetypal factory-assem-
bled thought, we may be able to grasp a truth that is of a far
more wistful insight into self: a truth that is not truth at all but
light into ethereal light that is the path of the mind and the
body as one working and harmonious constant.

Our lives are given over to meaningless pursuit and futile
chases after artificial dreams that we vaguely distinguish,
through the fog of reason, as our desires. We hold to our
desires as signposts to ultimate truths that we fervently agree to
and enact as systems of faith based on systems of belief, never
questioning our quick changes from one set of beliefs to
another, always sustaining our flip-flop values. Beyond our want
to believe and beyond our imaginations, we never feel the stillness of the self within us—that part that has no need to chase
and pursue nor to prove and defend. Indeed, we readily and by
the act of what we proudly name our free will, give the self over
to circumstances of proscribed duty: maelstroms of gross habit,
however tedious we find them, however mundane and however

full of suffering. With no question asked and without the slightest utter of objection, we surrender and reject what is most inviting in favor of matters that are much less. We are prostrate before our own burden and pain.

If we want to know, before it is too late, that what we see and hear and taste and smell and feel is real, then it must be through the realization of all sensory dimensions minutely interrogated, shaped clearly by the mind, correlated by the perceptive devices natural to the human body and in unison with that which is felt and known and that which is thought and doubted. Remembering is a function. Remembering is not thinking.

Such is the fold of the R.I.P. in the human fabric and this is the crux for topics of understanding, of perspectives, of passing things, transformations, value-to-value comparisons, and dialectical approaches to several novel concepts: *paradox reasoning, provoker function, impasse agreement* and, the solution, *impassionment of the senses.*

If logic is a method of ideal thought that is researched by introspection, observation, deduction, induction, hypothesis and analysis, then even these finely digested thought processes, within the glossy frameworks of implanted labels and symbolic meanings, should support active understanding of the piecemeal successions and lessons in trade for how many subscriptions, for how many ideas, in a steady, progressive stream of thought without bounds. Logic is referenced to this sort of progression only and not as a reference for use. Principles of conduct are applied to the progression of ethics. Principles of social organization are applied to politics. Reality in light of made reality is the method of metaphysics. The science and study of the mind is the category of psychology and philosophy. The method of entertaining existing knowledge is the contrived progression of epistemology.

Beyond such points of mental progression as these, there is the clear pleasure of reading into a finite self the tangible beauty that unfolds of itself as it is stroked and touched, decoded and released. Such unraveling of the progression of intention and decoding of the self in reason—for the release of feeling beyond reason—is *impassionment*. This is a step outside future past and into the being of now.

This discourse is meant to serve as a learning experience and it is not meant to enhance any already patronized and sanctified genre of thought; nor is it concerned with the catering to nor the glorification of a particular art nor adherence to any psychological, philosophical or political tracts.

The philosophical self was once a thing to be cherished, fully capable of setting forth a being of both rationality and feeling—one that could touch the essence of itself, that was filled with unending want to see and to touch and to know what it is, exactly, that encounters it, at any given moment, with stimulus received.

We are eternally pupils of nature and of the intrinsic self being that pushes us, through feeling, to the brink of reason and to the edge of desire.

We have created a fast-moving background and a merry-go-round in ersatz momentum. We are pulled into the spinning vortex where even the speed of sound is not fast enough, though we miss the point that, no matter where we look or where we turn, we cannot know how fast is the quickening blur. Indeed, it is hard to know the speed of sound when we so harken to it and are pulled by it; when we are lead by speed and propelled; when we are both bolstered and rent.

As we seek to detach from self many layers of what seems, at first, a mystery—and later is found to be masquerade—we discharge a variety of symbols, terms and meanings. As we penetrate closer to the self essence to feel, we passively connect with more codes and signs that are sensually enhanced or contained in internal messages turned over to passive memory for need with any subtle or sensitive use. Such intimately personal encoded messages make up recondite spheres of thin impulses and expose the precarious irritability of the raw synapses of self.

This is the fine netting of human neuron to human neuron that defines us, holds us within boundaries of diminished transparencies, and holds the inverted reflection of self. How hollow is life trapped within only a singular reflection!

Encoded devices cast shadow over all that is inherently rich in the human being and make plain the drabness of pre-meant values handed down. We exist in the shadow of descendent belief. Our world is manmade and handed down, but the being inside—the creature—is original and new. None of us fit well inside a world that is made and passed on through belief and obedience.

We have two very distinct information processing realities that overlap one another but are divided. The one division is of an active and focused mind of word implants that presage future past and are aligned with knowledge: the symbolic representation of bought tags to replace what we once held uncategorically and within human context.

The other side is a passively diffuse and probing mind that is willing to endure, even in the blindness of impasse in last reason, anything for awareness of the self that sees and knows the being of now. The rational root of thinking is revealed when all barriers to the passive mind are removed and deductive choice can deliver, intact, the images and emotion that are not merely a part of what is known by label and name but that which is, temporally, unknown.

Background knowledge is not the failsafe for genius nor is genius the arbiter of knowledge. Symbolic knowledge engages only background to manipulate and use. Both knowledge and genius are symbolic truths and both are conditional on reason. Knowledge is a symbolic instrument and genius is a symbolic myth. Ignorance is neither instrumental nor mythical but is solid.

Paradox, within the human mind, occurs when feeling, reasoned down to emotion without either being dismissed or deducted down to that which is in constant flux, is unrecognized by the senses and is ill-founded. This is false suffering. "To be or not to be" is no longer a question but a vagrant state of mind to overpower what comes next, and what comes next is fear.

The paradox in the mind begins as reason for or against an existent plan. We seek to disband, intentionally, any self stimulus that is uncomfortable. Active memory becomes a holding place for forward sliding intention. Provisional future intention must meet with intended results in order to make any annoying stimulus into counter reason. This is our failsafe for installing a working provocation. We purge last reason held and its false suffering; purge the unparalleled device that is part of our malcontent: to say "be gone" and to have it gone. Is not the belief in our false suffering the ultimate escape?

We seek to control. But what of the feeling attending such a move? What of that which cannot be controlled? Logic becomes illogic the minute that intention is aimed and directed. We attempt to force reason into place and we fall short of that which we intend. We try harder but encounter opposition. We have little control over the intentions of others in our lives no matter how symbolically clear we contend for meaning or how clearly we think we mean. As creatures of our own made reason, we are circumvented and impaired. In the pretense to evoke feeling from reason, there are impulses that we cannot suppress: dimensions of feeling that are free-floating and magnetizing. The sensual being defines and gives shape to the R.I.P. of paradox: it forms a sixth sense dimension within it. The creature becomes the beast with all senses working and alive—stimuli fully realized and references passively held—for feeling is ductile and malleable within mind/body continuum and space. The beast will not be deceived and the beast lives in now.

We may, in haste to reason, deem this feeling beast an aberration; a disgruntled affront to all that we have assumed to be manageable. The usual active remembering of what we have learned and what we have been taught and trained to exchange and manipulate as knowledge for commerce has nothing to do with assessing mind/body continuum nor with understanding natural breaks and schisms. It is hard for us, in mental slavery and deceit, to realize that there are no rules.

Prior to intent and after, sensual markings deliver feeling to the passive mind and are recorded in sixth sense, just as our taught responses are delivered up for focus in the active mind. Encoded with the internal language of self, the beast is always in touch with first voice emotion.

Since simultaneous recording occurs in two separate spheres of reality—written/verbal portrayal and its passive coexistence— sensual markings are further assembled and dissembled, interrogated and ordered for comparison and matching. The mind constantly looks for reciprocation. When all reciprocals can be matched, the beast is at rest.

A sea of consciously symbolic portents and signified things inhabits intention; is unresolved with the sensual beast and becomes paradox manifest: the human being constrained.

Within the chasm of unresolved paradox, there is the likelihood of emotional eruption which sensual markings, encoded in passive memory, try to amend. Such eruption of feeling is the voice and the movement of the beast that must, eventually, coincide with passive self memory: that which, in the throes of emotional upheaval, is then pushed in favor of intense want of reason as support for intent or as reason for reason. Reciprocals are in counter balance. Fear of the beast is warranted and conjoined. Fear of the beast is condoned and honored and given rite and ceremony. All matters of reason for reason are in honor of the pinioning of the beast. It is through the reciprocal of fear that we form our circles of blame and it is through loops of blame that we destroy our original self.

When we look at reason in paradox, we find reason for reason, which is circular in blame, and not reason to reason, which has no blind end. In the paradox of the R.I.P., all things are equivocations and they are equivocated as opposites. When reason finds reciprocal match within the passive encoded self, the corridors between the emotional storage areas, introspection and paradoxical slant, are voided. If reason paradox cannot be voided, there will exist a friction within the continuum of mind/body. Such friction is reciprocals in contention or duality of reason, impasse held. It is through self contention that we come to impasse, a plan-based justification made in order to satisfy a motive curriculum.

Reasons for reasons are stacked with intent to overpower the passive self that is held in contempt rather than to match and decipher impulses—to find them a place that has no blind end. We displace the enormous draw of stillness that is the passive self. We give credence to that which is inductive pretense and manufactured law and we disjoin from the broad side of our senses.

This is the R.I.P. in the human foundation that both impels and impedes us. This is the breach in the essence parallel and the R.I.P. in the universal parallel of consciousness which could make us whole.

The art enclosed within the pages of these written words accompanies the parallel of reason and feeling toward widening parameters to language and symbols that can open to display, unadorned, the human heart. Those things that can be told and those things that can live and breathe through the tenacity of flesh and muscle; through the pushing of self into self; and by the pulsing of blood through tissue; by their nature, become explicit breaking of form to deduce that which, for reason, has been induced in us. Reason deduced down to the beast is freedom.

Impassioned, the being sees through itself; into itself; and for itself. Impassioned, the being has no excuse. It has no failsafe for backward gliding into stalemate that is impasse and it has no excuse for the bludgeoning of the beast which is its own perfect self. Impassioned, the being has no excuse to destruct.

Originally, this was the purpose of philosophy: to evidence that man feels and, by his feeling, thinks and aspires to share the experience of feeling that is the gift of reason to feeling. To think is to question, and the answer to thought is no answer at all, but to learn the fine art that is ability to think is human-kind's original quest—his kinship with the beast—for original thought is not unlike the hunt.

The R.I.P. is the split in a perfect sphere upon which light is cast and shadow created: a defined silhouette that is the contour of reason. Distance is measured as time, spent and wasted upon a broken and contorted self that is broken by its trade, in bounty, for an irrevocable half life.

In half life, the self is squeezed and stretched for meaning paradox. In half life, such paradox cannot be purged. Reason and feeling cannot be joined.

The shadow of reason progresses until all emotional response mechanisms are failsafed to become perfect reason for reason stacking. The human being learns, then, to associate himself with the side effects of performance rated meaning for reason justified. Time is the perfect excuse for crushing so perfect a sphere as the human essence. Light is extinguished and self fades into encapsulated darkness housed inside the solidity of noun usage and inside the bleak assumptions of memory. This is the conscription of half life: I becomes We becomes They in a circle of blame. The agreement process fails while the standards of reason pursuit are raised higher to insure failure. Last reason held is the malignancy of the human mind.

Reason made is the second voice of half life. The human being has constructed an artificial being superimposed upon itself and he has assigned this being to act. Its acts are the ministrations of half life and it mimics life and mimics meaning. It subjugates feeling. It is bent on destruction. It consumes itself like the serpent who swallows its own tail, an ancient emblematic symbol of beginnings that have no ends. Artificial man, The Retrograde, is like a top that has no bottom; it refuses to admonish its motives and fears and sufferings.

Impasse is reliance on reason in service to think process. The construction of impasse is the false use of will. It is false because, in reason, the human being has no will because reason

There exists the contention, both biblical and inherent to Reason,
that there is a path or road that is, explicitly, the path of the Senses
or Feeling. On this path, neither Conscience nor Reason matter.
Both are abstracts that resemble Potential To Feeling as Feeling is
given Voice. Visually, we recognize this:

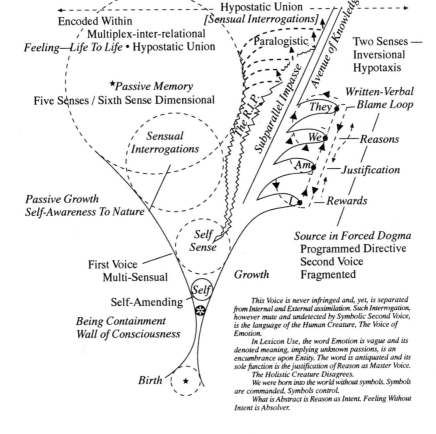

This Voice is never infringed and, yet, is separated
from Internal and External assimilation. Such Interrogation,
however mute and undetected by Symbolic Second Voice,
is the language of the Human Creature, The Voice of
Emotion.

In Lexicon Use, the word Emotion is vague and its
denoted meaning, implying unknown passions, is an
encumbrance upon Entity. The word is antiquated and its
sole function is the justification of Reason as Master Voice.

The Holistic Creature Disagrees.

We were born into the world without symbols. Symbols
are commanded. Symbols control.

What is Abstract is Reason as Intent. Feeling Without
Intent is Absolver.

is an artificial device. A prolonged state of impasse is failsafe for active intention and successfully blocks all sensually dimensioned information. In impasse, we claim the satisfaction of result rather than the full penetration of the senses. We have all been taught enough lessons in impasse to subscribe to a reward system wherein the greed of ego is paramount. Those who have mastered the use of impasse are rewarded for their ruthlessness while those who are at the mercy of constructed reason are fodder for supply and demand. No matter the cupidity of impasse, one who exerts it—and imposes—earns praise.

But impasse is a weakly constructed contrivance that issues paradox with reason amplified and feeling silenced to deter the unification of the whole. A powerful flux is created once feeling is cut off. The R.I.P. extinguishes the human being. It demolishes the self. What is mistaken for majestic will is the terminal illness of the human being. If the human being was in possession of will, could he elect his own self destruction?

The passive sensual network that is in want of accord is embedded in fixed symbolic representation that is a false self. The false self is the fabricated effect required to effect resultant ends. We impel our false self toward resultant ends for reward from impasse use. We are ward of our own false promise: if we suffer for our failure, this is false suffering.

In this study of the R.I.P., we are not concerned with why knowledge exists nor with the stacking of reason in intellect. This is a study, in thought, of how humans think and fail to think, feel and fail to feel, live in half life and fail to live. This introspection is a probe into the fragments of self and the ties that can make us whole. It is part of a transcending discipline that can encourage us into fresh realms and awaken us to the imbibing pleasures of all our senses. It is a look into the mental undercurrents of worlds inside worlds as they may be inhabited by us and felt and lived again and again.

In wholeness, we may see the traps that we set and that we help to set through participation. In seeing, we may encourage the careful consideration of others for feeling combined with reason—that others may learn that it is not necessary to separate them for reason appeasement.

As we look at problems that exist for the human race, we work toward a concise understanding of intellect and the evolutionary mental constructs that are, of it, defining.

To present an apt picture of intellect, we shall look at a collection of writing that we may savor side-by-side with art that is the flowering of this study, embracing a discipline that transcends knowledge for deductive growth. Art reveals the mind's ability to synthesize the encoded passive self, rendering images and symbols of feeling from below the impact of reason that are dimensionally defined, flowing always into the constant, into the now, felt seriously.

Ironically, one must bear in mind that the R.I.P. is an illusion and a part of think process that must soften and yield itself to passive analysis and digestion for it to become complete and a part of the intrinsic feeling self. Illusion can be matched and isolated within the human being. We use the very same forces of imagination and wit to create and destroy, to love and hate, as we do to think and make mean that which we deceive ourselves into believing is reality. Truth, as we know it, is based on this illusion.

Certainly we can benefit from what many philosophers and thinkers have tried to say and, there, left off. Even when they have missed their mark and never come to the point of that which they instinctively know and feel and deeply intuit, we can cull splinters of the self from their devotion to introspection and self sincerity. All thinkers pay dearly for their lives devoted to the probe of self. They do not find recognition in a marketplace that is no more than factory ordered, manufactured think-process of ideas for ideas and results for results in a jobs for jobs commercial milieu.

This study of the R.I.P. entails the *agreement process*; that which is promised that cannot be promised. The agreement process is the mammoth effort to preserve reason for reason at any cost.

Paradox resides in the mind as rift. We foster rift and division for blame and for payment in blame. As excuse, we hold forth the stresses of our lives and our overwork that brings numbness when it is we who have placed ourselves on this treadmill that will not stop. What will not stop is our perfunctory habit and our tradition of slavery.

The manner in which human beings think is doubt of that which is pre-meant and handed down. Need we accept the archetype as truth and homily? Critical deductive thought forges with the yield of passive self-interrogation to engage what lies beyond unauthorized mental peripheries. Beyond the outskirts of the mind are the portals that are the locked doors of intuitive creation. Upon the outskirts of the mind is a genuine love of self that can stroke the frail creature that can live without doors and walls—that lives within the liquid essence of self and close to our affectionate grasp if we so choose to touch it. It is the one thin light granted to us that we have been taught to contort and twist and maim and to all but snuff out. We die long before we die— before our covenant with life ends. What we call life is so thoroughly a waking death that actual death has much more to do with living than the sadly controlled lives that we agree to live. The agreement process is enactment of our prolonged agreement to fail. We agree to live our lives in reticence with our consciousness impaired and split to half life in exchange for hoaxed security, duty-bound love, the assumption of false authority and for synthetic values. We happily become living corpses in exchange for the promise of future life.

There is no future. There is no promise. There is only life that can be whole and life that is now. There are no chances to take and there are no odds stacked against others. There is only the timeless dimension of what lives in here and now and what is constant to the creature being.

To disagree is to know the opulence of self. To take steps outside of agreement is to move beyond factory-think knowledge that regulates and conforms us to technically reinforced and economically engineered failsafed acts.

The agreement process, enacted on multiple levels of society, is progress. The goal of progress is mass agreement on any preconceived idea that can be adapted as a way of life and is adapted, regardless of the loss of human dignity. Progress recognizes the value of ideas by virtue of their agreeableness only. However, agreeableness is dangerous, for as soon as agreed knowledge is enacted into progress, it becomes an empowered blind end. The followers of progress are indifferent to their altered mental state of impasse and their pursuit of progress for betterment becomes rigid.

Agreement for progress is the root of the quest for a future that is better and that will be even better when it becomes the best in terms of correctness and right. Such hope in future is futile and destructive. It reinforces paradox. Reason and intention become the word. Violation of the word is a threat to reason empowered and an act of war. Jeopardy empowered is the ward of blind belief and hope.

The R.I.P. in the human mind serves two purposes: justification of blame and the manufacture of words and slogans that connote and insure obedience, without doubt, to implied meaning. If progress moves along as smoothly as it can, no human being need ever be troubled by the need to think; for the connotation of thought is before him. Indeed, connotations are flashed and reverberated in the constant hum and buzz of media stimulation and simulation. The message is that one may wrap himself securely in the warm knowledge that a better and more right future is just over the horizon. The clear evidence to the contrary is a moot point. Pictures of havoc and destruction are commonplace, but the word is paramount and not open to question. We trust with our lives that which will destroy the human being: the word.

The vain hopelessness of future promise is lost on those who are focused, in active memory, on connotative meaning. Fear is the enemy. We gleefully trade self for promise, no matter the fallacy of such a hope nor its certain malignancy. The R.I.P. is the harsh penalty delivered for failure to live. Future promise pledges better life but it delivers an empty shell: an alien construct placed on the back of the frail being called human, the most gentle creature on earth.

Our hopelessness called hope shows in our fear and in what we mentally store and must come to draw down and to face. The dually matched justifiers, reason reciprocals, are as phony as the mental parody we use to portray cause and effect and question/answer bias. When these things are made to fit one side or the other, the tear will be mended, even at great cost in suffering.

Within this study of the R.I.P., we will touch upon certain acts of volition that might suggest human will or resolve, not as impasse nor any contention but a resolve that is without reason as a buttress. Resolve purges "to be or not to be" and purges all interrogation by interrogation. Question does not toy with dualistic justifiers but demolishes them and stops their momentum.

Man is a multi-dimensional creature in a mono-dimensional suit, clothed in reason and armed with intention in preparedness to defend tradition which is habit for resource and dogma, which is profit by belief.

It may be assumed that a skeptical man is a non-thinking and non-feeling man. An unrelenting skeptic has a mind that penetrates and probes. He is unwanted and is an unwarranted catalyst who pushes others beyond their usual limited mental states that impede real growth and resist change. The skeptic is too determined and set within a narrow range of categorical dimensions. A skeptic is a harbinger of negativity. His negativity belies hope and undermines promise.

But it is the skeptic who, by his negativity, is an original thinker: the negative one who asks questions that so disturb the hoax. For this, he pays the price of the outcast.

The skeptic is, first, an interrogator of self. He seeks out what underlies the vestiges of reason. The skeptic topples reason as the mental sentinel to the passive self that is the vessel for human dignity and grace.

Dignity is robed in tawdry vestments of truth and is interred in extravagant veils of deception used to justify hard-won seats of authority to acquire. Authority is the generator of blame and is necessary for empowerment of those in mainframe entity. This is manifest paradox with keepers of impasse.

Entity is comprised of representative think-processors for the masses of people who are not empowered—who are weak in either determination or skill or who prefer to remain blanketed in a false covering of knowledgeable security entrusted to the belief in future promise. Entity encourages non-involvement and non-thought for those who profess belief. This is the reward of belief. Profession of belief is obedience to ignorance. Entity engulfs all aspects of a culture, sweeps past and overtakes anything that could be left to natural human adjustment.

The human being fails because he is expected to fail and because he agrees to fail. For obedience to duty and for a dubious expectation of redemption from contrived failure, we falsely suffer and distort. We must ask: Is it more desirable to agree to fail or to fail to agree? For what, exactly, do we so despise the skeptic? Is it his freedom that we hate?

The use of think-process symbols as enactment for empowered truths has an obvious purpose: the advantage over others by commanded use of tradition and archetype. Youth is led to believe that love, favor and duty are cherished, natural elements when, in symbolic meaning, these things are agreement to never question and to receive love as favor of a share-held mindless duty for credence in right and good.

Deductive thought, the mental domain of the skeptic as empirical observation of what is humanely real, is not taught or practiced. What is taught and practiced are lessons in a made-meant-mean cycle of process-think for absence of thought and occlusion of feeling. The thing that emerges from such teaching is an indistinguishable part of an institutional muscle-brain. Tandem venture within a group structure gives the individual enormous faith in his own converted stealth and cunning. He believes himself fully capable of all cleverness based on reason for group manifest. All pretense to goodness and rightness for reason is laid into a think-housing word compound of what is assumed—and habituated—and what is made-meant to mean— and believed. All that defies belief is placed outside word compound and is held in contempt of reason.

Vying for position and for the spoils of conquest becomes of utmost importance. Submission for reason is the will to destroy. The R.I.P. is behind us and its shadow enshrouds our vested nature. Our falseness is failsafed and governed by the why of what may be called express lane truths. Blame and excuse justify excision after excision by their authority in justice.

Impasse is reason to failsafe last reason held, and then impasse is a final thrust for control. Impasse intends blindness for all but focused reason. Last reason is failsafed by why.

If human beings did not doubt at all, they would be able to assume things at face value. They could assume all truth and goodness and right to be as virtuous as they are touted. However, virtue exists only as manufactured; and it exists in causes set in politics and religion, and these causes are, undoubtedly, correct and true. Keepers of entity stack a subversive deck: one designed exclusively to preserve increments of power.

Religion fabricates the "don't worry plan" of noninvolvement and safe distance for the promise of salvation and heaven at no cost. Religion does not require self interrogation but promises an easy salvation, as though one may receive a stamp and be passed through the elusive gates of heaven as an empty shell; the more vacated, the better; no effective and working faith necessary; no illumination of self with which to contend. One is expected to serve a dormant self while supporting They induction and symbolic following. One can assume that the world of a blind man can disintegrate around him as long as his other senses are overwhelmed and unable to detect impending harm. We claim to want freedom and to have it: from what do we have freedom? What do we forfeit? Is freedom desirable?

Incidents occur daily that provide example of paradoxical thinking. Every incidence is cut off from another and from the cause and effect of each. The distance between such instances is filled with the clamoring for why. There is no piecing together of disconnected reason nor any unraveling of intention for the answer to the riddling of why. Humankind tricks itself into submission for reason and the wholeness of self is annulled. This is suicide. This is self-annihilation.

A minority rules while the majority trails along somewhere between "let's hang on for the ride" and "what are they doing now?" "They" are the holders of system-think logic with think-factory doctrine. "They" are the nay-sayers of what is now and has always been now. How simple it is to discredit the skeptic for his negativity when the positive is, so much, more precisely negative! They become we in subjugated impasse. We all know the uselessness of I.

Mainstream R.I.P. enters full-blown opposition to all that can be passively sensed. The R.I.P. opposes by intent to distort and divide. Doing matters more than not doing and, in R.I.P., progress and time are the reservoirs for useful work. Faster and faster we move with more of less behind us. We confuse symbolic teetering as momentum, consumption as progress, and duty with well-being.

It can be argued that action is always better than no action. Is it? Humans forget if given the chance to do so. In remembrance, fears proliferate and emotional wounds cannot heal. Forgetfulness invites rerun reasons and advances the absurd notion that, because one forgets, one does not care. Our assumptions about caring dictate that remembering is far better than forgetting and that doing is far better than not doing. But life is not lived in favor of singular memories and preferred reasons. What have the actions of doing and remembering to do with the deeply striking feeling of devotion to a perfect self that is supremely loving and innately tender?

Is doing better than not doing? Is promise better than even one audacious step "through the looking glass" of time and remembrance?

The R.I.P. is applied to all things that are remembered and done, even when they are done for the exactitude of duty only. What is forgotten and left undone is presumed to be of little importance, no matter the quick recognition of the eyes behind the eyes that speak more clearly than either the verbal or written word or any action based on duty.

We cultivate false hope and cling to group jargon for whatever may "stir the pot." Any original idea that is uncompromised is suspect; even as it drives deep into reasons stacked. To put forth anything that cannot be neatly agreed-up is taboo. We are rewarded for sublimation of self—to agree, to get along—to let authority intervene as we suck our thumbs and wonder at the control given; the power taken.

The stacking of reasons and the accordance with bland uniformity is voluntary. Sublimated will is the reward. Tranquillity of mind is the forfeit of self and the result of self forfeiture is the right of made-meant-mean intention in think-factory thought. We elaborately dramatize the working principles of reason. Man reasons and ponders his reasons, allows the machinery of the mind to move slightly and then, quickly reverts to produce a set of circumstances that are concurrent with cause and its predisposed and chartered effect.

There is no excused cause in the R.I.P. We trade our mental teeth in favor of softer food. We are processed beings living in a world of processed rules and processed dreams and processed hope.

Try as we may, we have not yet been able to process away the animal: our natural being. The beast is alive in us all. The tighter the noose about his throat, the harder he pulls. We have not yet been able to kill the beast and we cannot completely subdue him. What is it that we, so reasonably, fear? What is it that we take such pains to drape in the vestiges of knowledge and paradoxical agreement and impasse systems logic? Is it the beauty of our own illuminated substance that we have been taught to approach with fear and upon which we practice lessons of insignificant guilt and blame? To know fear, exclusive of reason, and to make it a friend, is to open the corridors to the dynamic self and the introspective sensual phenomenon.

If one has had occasion to listen to the faint beat of a heart near death, to listen carefully to this thing that is like a distant and uncertain drum, then one can understand well the cries of an intrepid and gentle beast. There are cries from humans that speak with the voices from dank reaches; from fields and forests that we once crossed for no reason at all; and to which we must, as mineral and dust, return. By the breaking down of the chemicals of our flesh and the falling apart of our fragile intellect, in the twinkling of an eye our lives are lived without ever having been lived. In death, there is no reason for pity. The pity is in our failure to live. The pity is in half life.

The R.I.P. is contingent upon ignorance and upon false levels of tolerance to the tightening of bounds. Paradox is the over and under perimeters that narrow and hold. It is a synthetic parallax that displaces and shifts two separate views into angular, directed points with meaning diluted and vortex obscured. Reason justifies and expands blame and excuse while passive feeling can justify nothing. Reason is an enlarged thing, its dominance based on conquest, on the braggadocio of what has been and what will be in constructed time to come through devout intention and proud objective for betterment of somehow, somewhat, sometime and somewhere. Reason is fortified by group cohesion to commonly held and traded beliefs, opinions, traditions and protected agreements. Only by authoritarian guard can the noose of agreement in reason be tightened. Only by absence of self or by self-abandon do we sanction constructs of reason that need validation.

We intentionally bury our thin and watery selves in solids that are as dense as granite and we admire the masonry no matter how grotesque the convolution of self, no matter the aberrance of our twisted beings who are in want of freedom from pain. We pursue freedom in alcohol and freedom in chemistry. We never pursue freedom in self.

We admire our reasonableness and pay homage to our heralded brilliance, rejoice in our quotients of intelligence; then we proudly display our neuroses as badges of courage and bravery.

No matter how happy we claim ourselves to be, inside our solid casts of factory-make, the R.I.P. remains in reason decay. We sense this in our contrite acceptance of mediocrity and we sense this in our willingness to deprive and to be deprived. We sense it in the split that we cannot deny. The R.I.P. is the gaping wound that, for reason, we refuse to repair. The R.I.P. is the fissure through which the human being falls, without once even touching the color and texture dispatched by the nerves of self. We prefer our safe numbness to feeling.

There is the impulse to stop, to give ourselves over to the caprice of completion. Feigning bewilderment, we do not question motion but allow ourselves to be propelled speedily toward time in future past. We reside in residuals. We can conceive the continuum of one long and unending day but we crave the acquisition of future relics sold by expert sale of noun/verb function. We hoard the products of linguistic prevarication for promise, as if we are incapable of our own determination of self and self constructs. The voice inside us—the voice of the self being, original self—intones the same message, and it is the redundancy of "a tale told by an idiot" and the myth of "tomorrow and tomorrow and tomorrow" when the perfect self is now.

The R.I.P. locks us inside the tragedy of not being and keeps us a single hair's breadth away from the magic of being: impassionment.

Blame is a profitable business. It R.I.P.'s the mind and plunders the human heart. This is the seal of political endeavor and religious zeal. Religion exacts redemption by a savior who is charged with saving both those who are blamed and those who blame, while utilizing the latter. Yet religion will condemn those who are without blame and without need to blame to exile in the word. There must always be arch sinners as there must always be saints in the name of hope. There is no such thing as evil except through reasonable and moral devise. A life spent on the outskirts of this premise often marks one as a traitor and as a paladin to a cause. Martyrdom is fraud. There are no saints and sinners and no saviors of our souls: redemption is now.

How can we amend a five thousand-year-old barter system based on the yoke and the plow, master and slave? Do we begin by giving things away and by making large, sacrificial donations? We cannot. Do we continue to buy and sell and to live the lie of goods that have no value? Is there choice? What is this thing that we claim to be our will?

We live in paradox and we live in the shadow of reason. By indiscriminate breeding, we are ethical robots. Political and economic inequities, starvation, pestilence and the suffering of the human being across the planet are either the result of faulty questioning or of no questioning at all. The timeless irony of "to be or not to be" is unconcern by reason. The question becomes, then, "What must we throw out and what must we agree?"

Hope is our eternal docility and the tractable method by which we sentence ourselves to the hells of our own making. Hope is the waiting for the nothingness in which we live to go away. Hope is bittersweet faith in stagnation.

We fail. Survival of the fittest does not apply. We are all quite fit to fail. If agreement is the universal signpost of intelligence for a species and, if we all agree to accept certain roles for the acting of agreed upon process, then let us act our way out of millennia of abuse and humiliation. Let us, by our exploits, remove the yoke of obedience and duty, remove the struggle between those who have and those who have nothing; for within this struggle for ubiquitous gain through numeration, we are assassins. We either idle in our ignorance or forthrightly kill by our forbearance. The judgments of tolerance are harsh.

It is our sensibility that reproves reason. To live in disregard of our senses is to live a life unlived. We condemn ourselves by reason alone. Death is not a choice.

Our antiquated systems of barter are falling apart. There is little room for consumptive gain. Boredom has reached saturation. Can we continue the perpetuation of self fear, sanctified ritual, biased sentiment, fawning adoration of self replication and admiration of the flimsiness that grants us passage into agreement? Are we satisfied with meager return for meager outlay? Are we content inside our failsafe of impasse and reasoned paradox? Do we squirm in the grip of an ancient vise?

We must ask: What defines feeling and what defines reason? Where does the vortex form? From what vantage do we trick the human beast into a life of suffering?

Originally, we are not the reservoirs of misery that we make ourselves mean and assume, through the profile of labor, as existence: the substitute for life. To live fully in our senses and in our sense to reason, we must probe the vast regions of self: "to take arms against a vast sea of troubles" that opens to the essence.

Future is a parody of history. The choice handed down to us through generations is what we may have that has been had. Knowledge is the tool of history and its repetition. Man is not what he cannot realize because he will not depart from the knowledge of history. He falls away from the very bones of his being. The mirror is before us but we will not enter.

Circumstantial impasse and the breaking of endurance come from the dangling of reward, held always just out of reach. There is a plentiful supply of synthetic distractions to discourage regard for perfect now. Bought and sold and delivered into future past, we disregard the parallel of feeling. The living planet is but a speck in the compelling universe of the mind.

Past is a parable fashioned for order and for the deposition

of future. All that "will be" are relics of the past. Future is artifact. Time is defunct.

In future past, failure is compact and complete; for that
which has been completed is set and does not change. We are
ordered into oblivion.

R.I.P. widens. Will and act, reason and intention, become
manifest as trades for empowerment inside the circle of blame.
Observance of duty becomes the test of group will that is made
to mean and made to intend future past. Act by group belief
becomes failure to act. Empowerment becomes success through
agreed right to fail or justice.

Empowerment is reasonable proof through reasonable goals.
Schools are merchants of immediate proof. Industries are merchants of guaranteed proof. Every purchase made is like a ring
of smoke connected to similar rings until it becomes a cumulus
mass. Such a toxic fog screens the natural ingenuity of the mind
and forms a uniform blanket of sameness and security. Power is
the will to self destruction. Encapsulated in time; wielded in
freeze-frame; static, disembodied, miscoded: What is called
power is like a virulent cell in living tissue. Pain is cancerous.

Those who have power through They Entity of group will well
know the want for power in the minions who vote and pray—
who endow their heroes and saints with a substitution of self. It
is not for mere drama that those empowered by group will use
the raised hand or clenched fist, for this is a universal symbol for
power. From our votes and our prayers there can be no fruitful
yield. Every savior is a disappointment. Group mind exhausts
itself in an inventive attempt to assuage its madness. There is no
winning side, for all sides fail and they fail by the merit of murderous intent; fail by the offering and enforcing of a one-way
path in and out of the labyrinth of lexicon knowledge.

Group psychology is grounded and fed on manipulated turn-
about and maneuvered flip-flop of ideations. It is not supersti-
tion that drives one into the flock. It is manmade fear. We fear
that invalidation by group standards will invalidate ourselves, yet

that which invalidates us for coherence to group consignment is exactly what points us to the path to the original self. Joining a group fortifies our mental muscle: I becomes We becomes They. We think that we are free when we have forged alliance with loyalty to duty. The group sustains agreed symbolism that is always subject to change without agreement, though changing to agree is commonplace and accepted. The deception is that there are no lies: all truths are valid by license and contract. Authorized use supercedes unauthorized disposition of self that is self in feeling, for feeling embodies no blame and contains no reason for right.

The concept of community is an enactment policy based on archetypal prescriptions and societal prototypes within the structure of a parasitic morality that feeds from hosts of its own creation and drives back any objection to its gluttony that could deter its set plan of duty for reason and reason for duty. Duty, as decreed by societal morality, keeps our noses perpetually to the grindstone with no recompense. Prizes are dangled just out of reach, like carrots before the donkey, to keep us moving within the snare of future tense. We bend and break. We lose our richness of self.

We are like dominoes, all in line: push one and all will fall. This is knowledge by agreement.

Peace and goodwill do not come from the strapping and binding to moral and ethical insistence but are born of passion and clarity of purpose. Those who are pressed too hard against life's commercial glass doors push hard in the vain hope of gaining entrance to a world of material comfort. This ramrodding tactic does not work; for all fall into the trap that lies within the glass, between the two plainly marked boundaries of have and have not. This is the split of the condemned unworthy from those who are reasoned worthy for their group-practiced correctness and right. The entity of the politically empowered pretends to equalize the odds. But if they did as they promised, they would not exist. Politicians are champions of reason conflict.

It is the theme of the correct that we are taught to crave
while we exist inside an impenetrable mental fog: antecedent
memory that dulls and binds. Every school child knows this: No
one cares for the child as long as indoctrination takes—as long
as ersatz momentum sucks him into performance ratings.

Our legacy makes us slaves to reason and masters of reason
and partisans of reason. We are stillborn inside the mental
womb.

The R.I.P. is the breakdown of fragility; the fragmentation of
regard; the cutting into two concise parts that could, as easily,
be left whole—one half that is devoted to calculation and the
other half for the dispersal of the ensuing haze. Conscious
memory is subconscious implant. It is a sub-parallel attended
only by sight and sound.

The human mind is a finely tuned recorder when it is
allowed to make palatable that which is felt. Reasoned with
specifically and without artifice, this sensual instrument can
automatically pull all order down into mental clearing. The
home of the heart is this perfect calm and to its home it will
return, whether in life or just before death: the being called
human will face itself. We all must speak to and break down to
the void. What, then, defines us? What is it that we so skillfully
dodge?

The R.I.P. invokes reason stacking; power-housing of I/We
complexities for future tense drive-line think factory that pulls
and tears at the being that is frail.

The R.I.P. executes blame cycling in made-meant-mean loops
of reason and pretends itself away from feeling and from entering emotional corridors. Justifying loops of blame become
adjunctive to the device of future-place holdings and invites the
masses to follow. Those who join rank are deemed flawless.
Those who refuse are failures by connotation.

What of those who refuse to play mental roulette? Do we
label them dysfunctional? Suffering from some traumatic distortion, hallucination, euphoria or despair? The hoax of reason

has hoaxed itself so many times that there is no conception of reality outside reason. In order to conceive a reality beyond all reason, one must remove oneself from it and pay serious penalty. Those who do not coincide with reason are considered freakish or cultist or, at the very least, eccentric. Psychological invention is capable of a sweeping devaluation of anything that comes in the way of agreed and failsafed reason in motion. Full value is given to all reasonable and governing intent for suppositious conscious growth and the hope for progress in future psycho-good. Nouns stacked on nouns call us to duty. The intention of noun/verb function as a device of factory think is to denote a manifested worth for the ordered symbiotic good of a group; but that is exclusive of common good. Understand and agree with group implication, buy its produce, sell its wares, enforce its imagined values and have reward: question insinuation and be cast adrift. Certification is by implication.

A biased faculty of what is good and right must prevail in a divided state of mind. No validated right can create blame without agreement. The essence of self, the creature, must not escape its cerebral tomb. Inside its casements of weighty solids, the creature, constrained, knows this. The silence of the human beast endures in aloneness, emptiness and sensual sojourn; waiting, listening and feeling until, through the residual vapors of fallen equivalents, it can find its own likeness. When we can find this, time ceases and we can enter the perfect now.

N O T E S

NAME: DATE:

II

II

VOLITION

Will Given Over to Word Manipulation

Who overcomes
By force, hath overcome
but half his foe.

—John Milton
Paradise Lost

DOES THE HUMAN BEING HAVE FREE WILL?

No; not unless he or she is removed from the truth that is connected within the agreement process. All other truths, being subjective, lie accountable to the self in periphery side effects: truth that is accountable to truth is no truth at all. The befuddled mind that is said to govern free will is reliant upon no self will at all. The befuddled and overburdened mind cannot, in one sitting, differentiate between rules and laws designed for blame, as the preclusion of free will and the intrinsic self that is the catalyst and crucible of free will and free range of thought.

Those who deny will in favor of an entity of we are favored partners in a protective agreement process designed and failsafed to de-authorize anyone who is not in synchronization with the boundary called impasse, the last reason held. Paradox must exist in impasse and it must insist upon the non-will of the many; utilizing a few elaborate and mundane devices built into a scheme that promises order through disorder. The failsafe in mass agreement is that there is no legitimate self-blame; for that is shrugged off as an impossibility, due to the forward of now mental state: intent. Future is not held accountable; for its motive is postulated as good; and good is not made responsible.

All that is not good is tagged, by entity, as uncommitted promise that is not formidable.

Progress, the stratagem that allows knowledge to hold sanctified reign over feeling, is, in light of that which is self, absurd and made idiotic by mass appeal for anything that can convey solid, mechanical truths, placed in noun/verb formats. Progress aligns itself with agreement that, the good of the group, is the right of the group to oversee, empower and protect the forward leaning truth; which both receives and sanctions itself. Progress is group agreement to do whatever is necessary to insure right over all claims to the truth of this social intention. Future is the word of progress based on a schematic promise to carry out future tense. Solid noun/verb usage, within a made-meant-mean system of label-think, provides failsafe to this burlesque of life, wherein assigned roles can be acted out and manipulated. Result is the word of the agreement process and the failsafe of knowledge is a ticking bomb set upon the human being. Tolerance levels are falsified through stacked intentions with fated assumptions.

False tolerance levels, to all distortion and bending of the self, are quietly allowed to build and stack one upon the other until no legal parameters can hold such weighty expansion of hypocrisy. Civil disobedience, as a requisite for change, is duly provoked. Pretense gained is far greater than pretense dismissed: hypocrisy is encouraged, even when we do sense and know that, beneath it, there is much more to realize.

Mankind may materially gain from the enforcement and adherence to such pretense; but at the expense of his own detachment from feeling and, in the long run, our children's children will pay the cost, a price set by those who cement their loyalty to the numbing duty of making life a business. Within this context, business is not the commerce of mutual trade but is manipulation that utilizes grossly unfair group tactics. The group tactics of entity promote a scrub life by allowing for a poor and meager existence at labor's bottom end. Some argue that this is the bottom that is necessary for there to be a top; or, they argue, that those at the bottom must have agreed to be there because, without that agreement, there could be no top or bottom.

But it is not a natural monetary squeeze that causes such a condition at the bottom. The root cause of top and bottom economic ends is social sanction implicated by group tactics or means to inhibit growth of well-being in favor of progress. Progress advances while well-being is forbidden and denounced. The social vortex begins its pull downward. Top/bottom arrangement forms a blame loop that is made to represent progression from one point to another. A sub-parallel labyrinth is used to simulate forward momentum as a suggestion of time progression. This is a false and humanely devastating tactic that is used to incite fluctuations of inflation and deflation, for the momentum that seals in fated consequence and devotion to unrequited duty.

The social vortex of group pulls even harder. We assume that future represents a forward aim—a movement toward someplace that is forward of now. The notion that there exists a starting point from which we can, then, move in a straight line to another point, is dubious. There is no place and no time beyond now.

Improvement sanctions discontent and, yet, discontent is always punished.

Word use gives us the illusion of movement. We reason that results give us a progressive hold on time. Yet, there is a final time when we cannot escape the fact that awareness is not knowledge and that intelligence is not memory. To insist that knowledge is truth is to insist that we know something valid in order to exercise right over cognition. Our agreement to the validation of truth and right and knowledge is our religion and we sell it to those who can remember it and afford it and carry it, for gain, into blame loop synthesis, the deceptive art.

Subconscious is a tool to perpetuate paradox. But all that we sell and teach and all that we have been sold and taught is not

nearly as fated as what we refuse to admonish by feeling, *a priori* of life: sensual interrogation and sixth sense reasoning.

We misconceive feeling as random hindrance and denuncia-
tion of reasoned intent. Feeling is human awareness embodied
in a single dynamic and rarefied sensation thrown into the
physical neural network for doubt; that is the cause of thought
and the cause of reason to form: reason, either to gather more
information and push feeling into voidance; or to take it
deeper, into Valhalla, where we can retrace the logic backward
until we reach the calm where natural fear impetus resides, in
peace, near the creature. One reason has voice and the other,
none necessary.

In describing will or the act of choosing an I approach to life
or a We approach to the tandem standardization of I, another
form of I or We begins. That which will always precede I is self,
and that which precedes the possible self is feeling: the sensual
channels held open to nature and, by nature, for natural
inspection and interrogation. I and We imposition is the lead-in
to paradox. Will does not exist by or for We pretext nor does
volition apply to a random and superficial introspection that
could become the subject of We without personification. The
embodiment of what could be called will is no more than self-
realized connection to place: the mind/body fullness as it
reaches to all aspects of feeling, and the recollection of what
sensual impact implies and impresses upon memory for information or cross-referencing for a continuing query that is of
and about life itself. What is makeshift will is a contrivance bearing manipulated cause and effect through an agreed and certified blame loop: a provoker function good/right theme that
provides appropriate schemes and advantages for group manifest authoritarian right and privilege to which one must subscribe in order to succeed. The social, mental vortex of reason
is formulated and paradox begins. There is no freedom from its
compression and pull.

In group manifest, there is no such thing as will. Will, in

paradox, is manifest We and is both prize and reprisal for the forsaken self. Impasse is imminent; and it will overwhelm the frail creature that is human. In R.I.P., it is but a dim possibility that any one human being can be a unique individual complete with working feeling.

The creature, human beast, whom, by the act of our agreed volition in group truth, we keep firmly shackled, is poised to take flight. His supreme anger is his strength to break chains.

NOTES

NAME: DATE:

NOTES

NAME: DATE:

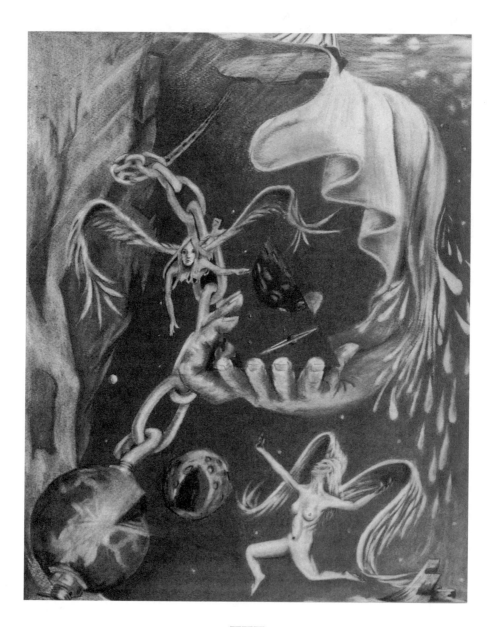

III

III

IT: THE VOICE

Sound: The Mental Scaffolding of the Subconscious

What began in fear and opposition,
became the Agreement Process; the single
most lethal action ever enacted upon an entire generation
in the name of civilized good.

—J. P. Beyor
Through the Labyrinth to the Invisible Self (Vol. II)

THE HUMAN MIND IS A MULTIFACETED and ambidextrous orb capable of assimilating impulses for balance, posture, walking, visual acuity and the delicate senses of taste, smell and touch. The human mind is capable of examining and identifying everything, within an introspection, so fast that there can be no computer invented that can do all that the mind and body can do with its vast cerebral network of impulses. The dynamics of the human being are always either entering new sensual/intellectual highs or succumbing to such exasperating despair that the existing knowledge, replete with taught mental impasse, is not able to rise above it.

In a traverse of the elements of speech, we strive to conduct our mumbling into mutually received and conjointly logical communication of tacitly marked sensual cues. Language is spoken, not just with words, but with movement and action as well. Words are the lowest and poorest denominators applied to the task of expression. Words are like empty shells that lie fallow and dormant without the full and combined use of our sensory perception—the satisfaction of minute and voluminous collections of information detected by the masterful skills of the five senses.

Speech is a culmination of sound that falls on the otic nerve. Sound interplays with continually incoming information that is absorbed and assimilated through all the senses for thorough cross-reference of tangible matter. Beyond that which is palpable through the senses is the luminosity of culminated perceptions: an ever-balancing wall of color and sound and fragrance and succulence.

What, specifically, are the properties of sound that cause it to fit or not to fit within the grand connections of sensual awareness? What credence do we give to sound that we do not accord to the other senses? What reason is there for separating the senses? How can one or two be placed above the others?

Before any sounds are registered as more than background noise, the brain must inscribe them into its vast body of intrinsic codes and extraneous, emblematic prototypes. It imprints them as vibratory intonations only, with pitch and meter undefined and diffusely connected to the harmonic whole of life. In such an undefined state, sound does not embody cause, but distills and dilates effect. Undefined, sound does not incarnate reason, but expands sensual stimulus. Purely received into sensory awareness, there is no ideation of want to disconnect it.

Sound, separated from its unnamed and unmarked whole, is isolated for the purpose of locating distinction and applying labels. Once distinction is made and labels are designated, there is the continual search for a particular corresponding sound. Once a particular distinction is made, separation is easily marked out and presented for memory enhancement, and what was once only sound becomes speech. Sound, then, becomes active memory processing of referred sounds. Sound is the original scaffolding of the subconscious. It is worth noting that the perception of vision is not similarly enhanced for memory. What is perceived visually is made manifest through speech and nomenclature. The eyes are treated as mere windows into the vacuum of what was once the complete sensual or fully-dimensioned self. There does not exist a purely visual language, for we name what we see with distinct particulars of utilitarian sounds. Symbols, then, only to vision and sound, represent instrumental mental replay. This is dualistic inductive increment for secondary exchange.

Sound becomes a jarring mechanism that is ignobly erected and contrived as word symbology, then, as knowledge, validated. Through the use of such base instruments of sound, chains of speech are formed from and for memory enhancement and manipulation of ideas. Through the use of matching reciprocal glossaries, tags and labels become agreeable terms. That which is retained in memory becomes subconscious affect. This is manifest tokenism. We are trapped inside label manifest for outcome.

The *agreement process* is enacted through sound and speech that are residuals of paradox think. The mind is, then, set in holding: impasse. Impasse is correct action framing.

We use the written word to express what is locked in impasse. Selection and distinction of sound blocks afferent cognition and maintains speech as the common denominator of knowledge in definitive and wanted circumstance. Knowledge supersedes combined sixth sense. The illusion of time and action becomes symbolic momentum, as circumstance becomes symbolic momentum. We automatically respond to and converge upon sound and sight that suggest movement: We are in love with action and speed. Momentum is the turning of symbols as though on a conveyor. Time is moved by verb until all practical language is transitory and vacuous, so quickly does implied and specified meaning shift. Jargon is jargon, no matter that it comes from the street, from law, from journalistic news or from electronic communication. Designer words are as fashionably fickle as designer clothes.

Memory is enhanced by the vibratory patterns of sound that imbue it with a self-assured existence in assumptive promise: One result for one effect. Momentum is favored for progress. Passive memory, still tied to the other senses, continues to throw information into the cerebral pot. The tracking of the external becomes muddled as the sixth sense matrix of touch, taste, smell and vision is overpowered by active memory pursuit of sound paralleled synthetically to word manifest. The ears, when used alone, are like blinders and mufflers: they impede the sensual being through selection of *a priori* half life information and assigned cohesive charge: the assured belief that words culminate and securely fashion chains of words and translate and transport artificially converging knowledge into resource, empowerment or resultant end. Tomorrow is future bright by disregard of all effective action upon accepted promise.

Words are but tiny props for support of the grand momentum of entity. Our labels are the names by which we deceive ourselves and with which we surround ourselves in a superfluous right and feigned good that is begot by manipulation accepted and in want to join and use.

Our pride in knowledge and our steadfast ability to agree becomes a mask for the searching, convulsing self, the thing that we seek to destroy through reason. In our dreams, we ache for the self that seems to elude us when it does not elude us at all; rather, it is we who will not come face to face. The R.I.P. is always present.

In repose, the sensual dimension claims the sleeping body with its assimilation and rumination of thought. We long for our dignity and of dignity we are unworthy. To know oneself first requires sincerity: The sapient specie is cunning and dividing even unto itself. In R.I.P., the creature, behind solid layers, is defective but is convinced, through agreement, that it is acting by right. Blame is manifold intent without concern for its actions.

Dignity is that which cannot be sanctioned—cannot be bought and sold nor propped up nor pretended. Our pride in the building of half life in word is willingly applied, by us, to the imprisonment of full life. The hasty taking of position, badges, medals, hats, crowns, certification and license appeals to our need for ersatz momentum.

Impasse has become so huge that the human being is dwarfed and humbled before the titanic presence of our own invention. We have built it well and made it sturdy: It can destroy us. It is hungry and demanding and employs sound as its ally and adjutant. Sound is the It and the Voice that controls and commands the minds of things: It demands agreement to its dominion. It cannot survive outside impasse. But it seals all exits from the noisy mouth of its labyrinth.

There was a time, some two thousand years ago, when speech and the reverberation of the written word had little value for persuasion and inveigling. As those charged with the authority of entity came to understand the use of language for the dissipation of individual will in favor of group will, language and speech became the postulates used to annul the human being. Tolerance levels could be stretched and pulled. The human being could be misshaped: twisted and contorted as reason could be moved about and relocated. The promise enhanced itself by following.

The voice of reason besieged the frail being that is human and cast it into a netherworld of made meaning and control. The more that this inferno was stoked and fed, the louder the treacherous voice of the moving it became until it made demands for place and position and status. Sound and momentum became the glory and the power. Man was moving, and moving in speed was rapture. The world has not been the same since the voice became It and It became paradox.

As the sound of the voice of It increased in volume, in speed and acuity, those who professed love for its noise were given ancillary jobs and a share in the agreement of future promise. From a proud and errant seed grew a many-tentacled spectacle wrapping its coils around the essence that is human, wringing it of its natural gentility and replacing it with the deadness of compliance. Brave by reason of size and bold by reason of authority, it gained control over all new sounds. Meaning became aligned with motion, speed, consumption and power.

Voice tagged and recorded new symbols and saved them. It
wrote its own excuse and called it history, rife with half fact for
designed truth and innovative lambastes and censoring jargon.
It learned failsafe. It, as entity, sought reprieve and salvation
from its own plunderous bargaining and smarmy promise, and
it granted itself, in agreement, such relief. The voice of It justifies and redeems itself always. It takes no blame but assigns it.
Without blame loop, it falters. If paradox falls, entity will find
more powerful bromides with which to brand and subdue its
miscreants.

In the twentieth century, It evolved, through technology, into
a thing of unprecedented entitlement. It could move at the
speed of sound itself. The voice of It became as close to its subjects as a local television broadcast and as intimate as a video
recorder. Endless pictures of widespread waste and desolation
inflicted by the voice of It flashed and blinked and crackled
from all appliances of broadcast media. Pictures became the
word. The voice of It soared above the minions who adhered to
its oily promise and agreed to its purpose and, yet, mourned
the loss of their volition. No vote could appease it and no
prayer could temper it.

Intention and duty to intention confirmed synthetic time. No
longer did the voice require sanction. It became sanction and it
decreed sanction and bequeathed it. The voice, as function,
became its own failsafe.

Falsified paradox is impasse, last reason held: It is the voice
of last reason. Last reason is reason extinguished, and the middle will not hold.

Fear of the unknown is the shame that becomes reason. What
is more deafening: Secret voice against silence or secret silence
against voice? Innate fear is automatic and unconscious. Fear of
fear is exponential subconscious knowledge and fear of the
unknown, then, is a semblance of knowledge: impulsive, slick
and cunning. With its own primordial pool, it is a merciless
predator.

Fear that is without disclaiming fear is the interrogative of self. Fear is the question mark that is the key for opening all shut doors. Fear is friend to the beast and its liberator. Fear is friend: To walk through the doors to self, one need only touch it. By opening the doors to self, what would be fear is not fear, for it is through fear that we question motive when impasse reason is challenged.

Does religion encourage us to interrogate ourselves through natural fear or does it reinforce the barricades of iconic fear? Is religion about God or about the implantation of iconic fear? Does religion embrace fear of the unknown as misrepresented fear of another implanted counter-fear—for use as a saving grace and a hooking promise for those who think that they need a safe anti-fear religion and a god of resignation who can subdue interrogative fear—without, even once, getting close to the one complete sensual self?

Religion makes things easy: Design one word for one flat dimension and one salvation by subjugation to duty; split the creature into two dissimilar and opposing halves. Blame is for profit.

Religion is paradox ideated and We personified.

Does politics protect the welfare of the few for the common good of many or does it provoke timid citizens into civil disobedience merely to keep themselves from being pushed too far? Do politicians hastily depict goodness and correctness with a quick change of hat or position or service to words? Does politics thrive on fear of the unknown or subconsciously implemented fear of fear as an impetus to vote? What are the fears that are sold back to us as overseers of our fate? Do politicians urge us to war only for our own killing urge? What shape has political jargon? What sound does the voice provoke in us? Does fear remain as friend or foe?

Politics is paradox with weapons drawn and muscle at its command. Blame loop is nearly exclusive to the machinery of war or police action.

The matching of natural fear to implemented fear is *provoker function* or impetus to obey. Fear is inverted so that what we fear subjects us. The job of religion and politics is to provoke habit into duty, reason for reason and result for result. Without provoker function, blame cannot form a closed loop: impasse. Fear of fear and fear of the unknown insist upon blame in lieu of discovery. Anti-fear becomes reason over reason. Think-factory process stems from the provocation of reasoned blame thrust, strategic advantage and a working hypocrisy.

Knowledge is impasse by paradox.

Reason is failsafe to paradox.

The agreement process is paradox.

Can there become a disorder of convention and still remain an order that unifies? Disorder heightens the realization and execution of paradox and justifies it. Truth is the validated means of production and the share-held impasse of I-We-They: Entity.

Can the realization of locked paradox forestall a chain of events linked by ever-mounting stores of failsafe, blame and ever-thinning false tolerance levels?

Paradox unrealized is paradox installed and set. Patterns of events are set in paradox. Truth benefits from sets of facts made for truth. Replay for replay alters nothing. We live suspended in an altered state: Fear is not our friend and words are our deceivers.

Events that have become set in the linkage of paradox cannot be stopped. Is there an alternative action?

It is not action nor speed nor sound that is needed. It is not impetus to function nor any provocation.

We live in a state of disjoined parallels. Nothing will happen that does not first happen in feeling. If reason fails feeling and feeling fails reason, we will continue half life in paradox with failsafe entailing, and the voice of last reason will be the last voice of blame.

Blame will be the voice of the next logic-illogic and its pitch and its frequency will rise until its wail stretches boundaries of tolerance to the point of shattering.

When the human being breaks down, the sense of hearing is the last sense to fall away. When we can no longer hear above the ultra-high frequencies of paradox, our undoing, as a unique specie of creature, has begun.

Universal parallel of consciousness must be rejoined and the wound of the R.I.P. healed or it will be misshaped into a sub-parallel of irreparable despair.

The pretense of allowed involvement is not subject to caprice. It is a "get away with" attestation for joining cause and it is the reason that fear causes belief. Is it feeling, thrown back to self-interrogation, that defines the cutting edge of fear, or is it circular reason at the center of a circular maze, a labyrinth of made-meant-mean sub-parallel subconscious demoralization of self? Words carry impulse. Our invented manifest reality is noun/verb false reactions.

If stripped of reason, the human being would be inanimate and mute. He could then, in his silence, know that reason is performance and expectation of performance. He could understand that speed and momentum are connotations of mock time and mock progress.

What if performance could be pulled from reason? Could there then, both in fact and in pretense to fact, remain a memory-enhanced active feeling that what is missing is not performance at all, nor deed, but calm? Could it be that motion, as the means for approaching some distant place, is in active want of elapsed time to travel, a defined axis between stillness and motion, between stimulus and no stimulus? Can elapsed time, then, be defined as active memory? If time is defunct and future an artifact, where are we going? In stillness, we are going where we are now. We are, outside time and without future, our own memory.

The insistence upon crossing distances is measured in and by reason and in terms of false wants.

Must we forthrightly blame all that is silent into motion whether we want to or not? Must we eternally kick the bees' nest to know the fury of the stinging bees?

Motion is a steadily accelerated force exerted on or for or against an object or a conviction. Nature has a sinuous undulation; a cadence that we cannot decipher. It pulls and does not push in its sway; it is silent.

We are the voice of It and the voice of the We of They. Our duty to entity is our sacred reason, and it demands every morsel and every strain of self to be delivered.

Without the clear self-inherent sounds of all our senses overlapped in dulcet unison of one full voice, we can never become silent enough to know the calm inside. We need not exist disjointed in the dark hole of the R.I.P. The subconscious subparallel of the word can be felt and dissolved into one voice with interrogative fear as its friend in universal parallel of complete thought.

There is a quiet voice that turns the human essence over and over again until no turning is necessary until, stillness to stillness, parallels are blended.

Fear is the teller of circumstance: emotionally enhanced in the full life and freedom of the creature, the most gentle and loving thing on earth.

NOTES

NAME: DATE:

IV

IV

PROVOKER FUNCTION

The Good of the Few Over the Many

. Words strain,
Crack and break, under the burden,
Under the tension, slip, slide, perish,
Decay with imprecision, will not stay in place,
Will not stay still.

—T. S. Eliot
Four Quartets: Burnt Norton

WORDS ARE DESIGNED TO REPRESENT PARALLELS between subject and a visual communiqué of subject which, when translated into the symbolism of language, becomes the product of proposed description. Words are intended to convey description of matter.

Everyone knows that green trees are green. Green is representative of what the eye sees. But the eye does not see green and it does not see a tree. It sees an object that is named "green tree." Is green tree green and a tree because of words? No: This is only a frame of reference that employs the nomenclature of a given language. The ears receive a token euphony: The sound of green tree does not connect to active memory until the appropriate visual image is cogitated. Only then may we move to the visually received subject and say "tree" and "green." We mentally connect imagery to the process that green and tree must represent what we perceive. Does this mean, in conversation, that we may say "green tree" and everyone will know what we mean? Unless everyone has seen a green tree and associates those words with the given subject, this cannot be so.

Is green tree a green tree because sounds intoned in the throat match visual assessment? Vaguely, this may be so, but we need to also imbue the visual image with the textures of touch for full sensual configuration. Add to those dimensions the spectrum of fragrance, and we may be able to present something that can be agreed by all to be green tree.

Yet language is devoid of smell, touch and taste; it must wallow in filmy dimensions of flattened likenesses.

Everyone knows that the words "green tree," with the shapes and the textures and forms that are simulated, can be referred to and agreed upon as symbolic of identical or similar things. Through words, we may conclude the Agreed meaning of green tree. We may document its meaning as determining information and finalize it by printing it into a dictionary of Agreed definition. Through the final act of printing and binding the written word in book form, we establish Agreed fact for base recollection and transfer of flattened material in symbolic form. Function and use are accepted to make mean the symbols and propel them as provocation to recognize and sanctify made fact.

Imagine that a child lives in a desert that is barren of all trees and barren of all but muted suggestions of green. This child has never seen a green tree. Is it possible to stimulate his senses into evoking green tree, even assuming that spoken languages are the same between the child and his visitor from another land? Is it possible to convey to him the full thought of green tree without drawing a picture or diagram?

This could not be possible since, through the use of language alone, the child could have no sensual reference for knowing green tree. At the point of learning the words green tree, the child's senses would naturally question the meaning, but without access to full sensual awareness, he could have no way of realizing, beyond mat provocation, the thing that is called green tree.

Without integral demarcation of all sensory stimulus, nothing can be told of green tree. Without parallel match sensory associations, symbology alone cannot be understood. We merely parrot taught labels and pass them off as meaning, either by implication or specification. What is of natural, external cause and effect is remembered and pictured in the full scope of an intrinsic sensual language that contains the dimensions of sight, sound, touch, taste and smell. Through these five senses, we are able to enjoy a composite Sixth Sense: the initiate whole parallel of consciousness.

Ponder the silent dynamics of these five inherent voices as they overlap to render sensation and emotion. Consider, then, exactly where they are stopped and provoked for Reason and for function. When there is external reference through sensual understanding , words, as representatives of objects, fail. Rigidly controlled recognition of fact obligates us to the use of obscure gestures as substituted excuse for perception that yields a drab, mechanized picture. In sensory delineation, there is no final definition but biologically encoded impulse without name that is felt into place and stored within an emotional manifold of passive memory: place where time is artifact. That which is passive in the mind constantly renews, washes and bathes itself in multiplicities of pulled down rationales that dissolve words back into the original language of Self that existed before the world of the human being was separated and The Creature held captive in active memory.

The tree pictured in the mind as recognized fact does not have color. Color is external but, in the imagination, it is superficially represented with given verbal implication. Without stimulus, beyond language, even the shape of the tree may be confused with other representative shapes from our base lexicon. There is a loose connection that forbids us knowing green tree: We neglect sensual determination. Without it we assume, through mutual Agreement and distribution of Agreed fact, that green tree exists. We can look through a book of reference and find a description and even a color photograph that imitates green tree. However, the subject remains dim and elusive. Through pictures flattened in a book, we can know only a single plane that is devoid of quintessence, visual metamorphosis and palatable taste. The mind cannot completely "connect the dots" and is left with only a bare outline. Through singular or secondary dimensions, we have only subaltern or tertiary insight into color and form. Yet we have come to tout and sanctify this flat-line excuse for knowing as Knowledge; and Knowledge in Paradox is rewarded no matter the ignorance of it. Memory is Knowledge and nothing else; memory is not intelligence.

Unless we physically engage and sensually interrogate, we store only flatness. We store even ourselves as flatness—as vague connotations for what we are and what we could be if memory was not glorified. Memory has nothing to do with Full Life.

In language, we may assume either vague partial reference, which we call connotation, or reference by Agreed specifics, which is denotation. This is where sensual interrogation stops. There can be no such thing as either a denoted or connoted green tree. This notion is Agreed fact distribution that is based on the impressions of memory. The word, as memory, replaces the fleeting reality of sense.

Trees are trees in form, and green is green in color and in shade of color. The interpretation of these things is no more than a sensual window. Bilateral sight and sound imply combining representative meaning by sub-parallel diffusion for word and voice transference only.

The living thing that we call green tree is innocent of being anything at all. The thing that we call green tree just *is* and we are grand inquisitors of what is. Without humility or even question, we widely distribute vague impressions as fact. We tag and label and forget, through memory, the origin of thought and adapt our impressions as made meaning with barely a glance at exactly what we deface and devalue through words in function to provoke.

Sensual materiality is reduced by Agreement and by reaching imagination. We label and tag and affix implied meaning to things that are well beyond our comprehension—things that are beyond words and beyond formulae for knowing. Yet it is with such flat labels and tags that we define and rule our lives.

We allow the pretense of words to suck dry the vigorous essence of Self until it is withered in beauty and without deep emotional feeling. All that can remain within this shell of memory is the explicit danger of deceit.

Provoker Function is a validated estimate of *Agreed Flat-Line Knowledge* that is granted unquestioned credit and trust. Provoker Function purposely finds that which could be refined and magical and levels it to a smooth and tasteless mediocrity—lays to waste completely even the possibility of original thought. Within the context of Provoker Function, the sensual embodiment of green tree is encased in one common husk that contains no meaning except that which is made. We could write a thousand books and never come close to doing what the senses can do in one fell swoop; no forefront active imagination necessary. The sensual matrix of a completely open and feeling human being is beyond all imagination and beyond all symbolic abasement. The Creature, in zero space, has no fear.

Our efforts to describe green tree can only result in suggestion and insinuation and proposal, for language cannot match the original language of sensual contact. In the distribution of whole blocks of lexicon, we must ask ourselves: What is it that compels us to function and for what intended purpose or gain?

The negative serves more than the positive. We relegate feeling to happenstance and regulate Reason to rigidity.

Denotation is the rationalization that we may elicit and educe the entirety of green tree to reason and know it through the Agreement of language. This is the ignorance of Retrograde, the sapient. In Paradox, we condense the far ripples of our astonishing selves into tiny, collected remainders of processed flat-line thought.

Connotation and denotation are amalgamating links in the Agreement Process and cannot deliver dimensional material to the total being. We are overrun with formidable, condensed impressions packed tightly and heavily weighing on the frail creature that is our original Self. The fully living and sensing being requires lighter fare than the bogging constrictions of implication and specification for identifying and defining the things in its world. The sensing human being requires a practical understanding of green tree as a unique and interesting structure that cannot be redeemed through connotation and denotation. Life cannot be redeemed by word in Half Life. What is real is real by feeling and by cognitive first impression passively displayed only as it is sensed. Meaning does not exist except as made; for only the combined grasp of Sixth Sense can understand feeling that demands no feeling.

Comparable to the flat definition accorded to green tree is the more seriously censoring dictionary definition of Conscience. Its meaning in Agreement is: "The sense of what is right or wrong in one's conduct or motive, impelling one toward reaction. Ethical and moral principles that control or inhibit the actions or thoughts of an individual. To feel guilty about something. Certainly; most assuredly; without doubt. Knowledge. Awareness." The implication is that We must be right and the specification is that the sanctioned We must control and be controlled by Entity in order to be right. If We are right, We need not be bothered by guilt for, through use of word control, We are absolved of Guilt. We are rightfully inhibited and morally ethical—without doubt, through Knowledge.

We Agree to be right. If we Agree to be right then we are right. If right is intended, we cannot be wrong. Only by Agreement of the group can we be said to be wrong. If green is validated green by the group and tree is validated to be tree, how different from this is the concept of wrong? Can right be explained to the child in the desert any more convincingly than the concept of green tree?

This is the language of subconscious sub-parallel dictum. The language of sub-parallel provocation pulls the Self away from all working sense and passive memory comparisons and checks. The reality of subconscious thinking is no more than a provoked made-meant-mean state of Agreement. The word conscience is taken from the word conscious, defined in dictionary meaning as, "Aware of one's own existence, thoughts and surroundings; fully sensitive and aware." We are taught the lessons of conscience while whole consciousness is shoved aside and sensitivity is depicted as slovenly, wasteful and weak, its deep emotional language enveloping The Creature.

Through the connotation and denotation of conscience, we are delivered into active service and duty to Entity of the altered state that alleges unconditional promise for a share in promise to deliver the goods of Truth. Truth is the right—the key to hold warrant—with Agreement made loyal to Duty only, ruthlessly dominant by the artifact of Intent.

Provoker Function is the attempt to define and separate good and bad without sensual participation. Separated senses are used as a convenience. Intended meaning for Reason leaves nothing left to sensual investigation. Can a conscience exist if one is consciously aware to the point of non-doubt? We must ask: What are our sensual dynamics? To follow and Agree and to share-hold the separated benefits of mono-frame results is Half Life.

The implication of conscience provokes an individual to perform according to and with allegiance to Agreement Processing for Knowledge enacted by job function or religious or political promise. This is belief warrant: Provoker Function controls and inhibits thoughts and actions. This is captivated fulfillment of a subjugated Self in unconcern.

Are people aware of their existence? Can they be consciously aware when the average person can carry conscious thought for less than three seconds yet carry charged symbolic provocation in memory for resultant end cause day after day? Have we provoked ourselves, by design, to follow blindly without question—to simply obey the order of words and to acquiesce to their authority over dignity? What percentage of world population holds the key to manifest word authority?

What is it that our anxieties carry? Feeling is emotion. Made guilt is connoted symbolically to provoke one into intended act in order to hold to Agreement through pre-thinking good, bad, right, wrong fact for distribution to a ready-made Truth derived from Agreed resultant ends serving Entity manifest. Our truths sadly lack full rational sense, so immersed in duty have they become. We define them in flat-line unadulterated planes. Those taking their charge from Entity's promise rather than from self-awareness have no choice but to use conscripted terms and jargon for Blame. The thinker does not use jargon for Blame, but thinking critically from his own specific meaning, he Blames himself. Those involved with the use of Entity Provocation in Blame are frightened by individuality.

Provoker Function uses perfect Blame Loop to persuade Agreement to a think-processing of noun/verb compounds. From the subconscious word labyrinth and the symbolic sub-parallel, we become character actors and players in a tale of subversive regulation. Loyalty to Entity is rewarded with benefits: The more snugly fit the blinders, the more rank and privilege.

Can it be necessary to wonder why some people commit suicide? What seems normal on the outside is a maddening fury on the inside. The thinker is First Voice active encoded in Doubt and continuous transition. The Creature comes to a brink of intolerance from laboring to register abstract intended meaning, serving only singular reactionary causes. He sees the unbalanced facade all too clearly but cannot get through the guarded labyrinth. Some bend under the strain and fold into the soupy mass, virtually foregoing the Self. Others so loathe and disrespect this manufacture of reality that their beings cannot tolerate the pain of exchanging feeling for rote enactment, and they are consumed. The Creature is not insane but is tender and amicable and afraid: He Blames himself while society delegates Blame and smashes its members.

Anger is the outcome of the altered state. In suicide, anger is directed inward and, instead of taking the life of someone else, one takes one's own. In this way, one spares oneself: One spares oneself the pain of hypocrisy and existence in Half Life next to it. There are many cases in which children are killed as part of the parent's suicide. This is done to spare them the same sensed agony in Future or to prevent them from having to endure years of battle with a two-faced reality of flat distribution and use.

This study is about what is obvious—not what is abstract. This is serious when we consider the worth of lexicon in the long run under intended good and right. We must ask: What good is a good that is misfit to the dynamics of an emotional creature?

As tolerance levels are stretched and impaired more and more, the composites of humanity recede and feeling is forced into the background. Feeling is the unfit language of now, unassigned and silently menacing to Future. Confusing and always changing strategies, diabolical motives, and the sheer exhaustion of trying to "keep up" and "make do" designate suicide as an only out. Suicide is an insalubrious and calamitous choice, but the human specie is tethered completely to its reasoning faculty. Other creatures would not tolerate the emotional cage in which we place ourselves: They would bolt from it! The human being often favors blind choice for blind choice, for whether real or imaginary, Reason is an infraction placed for subjugation. It is a promoter of mass promise and ideal. Reason is a harbinger of Future Past and of Redemption Tomorrow.

Reason deceives us and supersedes feeling that can know the inner working manifests of man and woman. Emotions are foreshadows and tellers. When unavowed feeling builds and falls over itself, tolerance levels have peaked. Overextended and circumvented tolerance levels produce superficial cause by mounting singular effect as a warning device. Such unrest is not strange considering that the hard thrust of Reason Pretense relies on the subdued and yielding tactility of the human being, always an easy target. The majority question it only under their breath.

No one individual is singly responsible for allowing that

which exists in deadlocked commonality. We are all constituents in Blame for job accommodation and life lease. We promote by silence and we condemn by our silence and our complacency. We live out a redundancy of atonement that is long overdue for expulsion from the human psyche. Too willing are we, with our silences, to lay our destinies at the feet of mythical heroes and inquisitors whom we want to make believe into an ultimate accountability. We long for our Alexanders and Khans and Caesars just as we condemn them in History. As believers in virtue, we deny our brutishness in precisely the same manner that we condemn it to Reason.

It is through silence that we are responsible for denial of life and we are responsible for the rending of Self. Within our Agreement, we fail, and within our Agreement, we enslave. In Agreement, we dare not claim an eye for an eye and a tooth for a tooth. We forfeit our primordial animal Self: a sweet-natured Beast who is, to the Now, self-adjusting if allowed to adjust; The Beast in Now is The Creature unleashed. We prefer a method of Provocation that is mechanical and reasoned slick. We slaughter nevertheless, with slyness, loyalty to Duty and group cohesion. Inverted, we call this enactment of freedom and justice.

The religious sword, righteous tool of nondescript believers, would zealously strike down such Provoker Function and still lay claim to a nemesis with which to contend. The hypocrisy of religion is that it is both friend and foe—both pantheistic defender and upright crusading ideal.

Religion share-holds the same Blame Loop as politics; but at opposite ends. Politics toys with the middle ground as its yo-yo. Political testament, by use of Reason devoid of feeling, trains its partisans with a shadow-box trick: substituting dimension with intention, penumbra with sparkling light, tomorrow for sad tomorrow where intentions meet.

Politics parlays to a winning side. It says, "Give us your fears. We will paint them and spoil them so that even you cannot recognize them. Then, we will return them to you as promise.

Make your wagers: Any way you bet, you lose."

Factual truth is Belief made to represent itself for Reason alone. What becomes existing circumstance is memory-adapted change: Impasse. Reciprocity in Paradox is Reason held for Reason used.

We are subjugated by dangled illusions of grandeur in trade for resolute sensual awareness and the concord of a perfect Now. We possess, already, what we seek, but it is too calm, too beautiful, too serene; so we deny it and disown it for a rush of speed and future and prayer—momentum: the make-busy of Self-undoing.

Our good pietism and our good citizenship prolong the misery of the human condition. We are our own dumping ground and our own unconcern. We invent misery, then pretend to cure what others are made to suffer as outcome of our sapient knowledge and progress. We bend and wax and play with words in order to veil the ruinous havoc culminated from degenerative and failed logic. All labeling stems from a common source of partial fact. Can we be sure of all that we see if all that we see is the placid result of partial fact?

Partial fact becomes Agreed Truth. Agreed Truth becomes Agreed Rule. What is green tree? What are we provoked to see? What are we made to believe?

Believers/Disbelievers contend that abstraction is difficult to assess. Yet these same enchanted/disenchanted conjure up their own exclusive imagined place and set it next to a better place complete with a God remote from a Now being. Even the promise of God as doer is a broken promise.

There is no such thing as abstract feeling—only the wash of discarded Reason returning to the place that is defined and dimensional within the sensual Self. To disown feeling by Belief is impossible. Religion asserts that the human being is complete in every way as long as he clings to a controlling dogma and an iconic redeeming savior or the tyrannical God of dominion. Religion dictates that, through Belief, there can be no need for abstraction though the very harsh and brittle "realities" of our world impel us toward disassociation and alienation of Reason. It is a natural human motive to move toward what is abstract: that which has no earthly name and that which has no control; that which defies Belief. Yet it is just as much a matter of urgency to respond to uncontrolled abstraction as it is to adhere to the rational. To complacently ignore the abstract is placated Reason, nevertheless.

We have no inborn capacity for the incessant naming of things. As young children, we see things from a very broad spectrum. Everything that we see, hear, taste, touch and smell is part of a panoramic abstraction. We are involved fully with the spectacle but can easily walk away from it once intrigued. We feel almost exclusively in subjects that are sensorially real: color and vibrant imagery, enticing smells, melody and textures.

If we are left alone to name an object, then, we give to it a name that becomes a part of our own particular Self definition. Young children have little or no association with prescribed Intention: They have no Reason. They have no patience with Reason as meaning. If, as adults, we can move aside the set denotation and connotation of things or set meaning, we will later describe such a moment as an epiphenomenon. In childhood, all experience is phenomenal and epiphenomenal. We know nothing else because our minds have not been symbolically composed and our sensory mechanisms are wide open. We may call this openness Sixth Sense: the language of Self, the sensual being. Memory, outside time, is holistic and immediate—not fixed by effect to a cause .

Sixth Sense is quite different from Reason Pretense. It seeks satisfaction from total voidance of justification and pretense in Reason. The passive Self pulls Reason into the harmony of Self constantly. But the unraveling frightens us. The Perfect Creature lives in this neutral place beyond Reason. In R.I.P., place is severed.

Sixth Sense is the total being seeking serenity beyond the

scope of Agreement that is dominated by two senses—hearing and seeing—and beyond Future Past, the circumstantial demand. Sixth Sense is the total being seeking serenity in the abstract of Now deductively and sensorially—not inductively and knowing.

The Sixth Sense of the total being does not know symbolic green tree nor synthetic consciousness nor labeled conscience. Such concocted terms are wrought with pressures and over-simplifications that inhibit and weaken sensory intake. It is the Provoking impetus of word imposition, inductive memory loading, and their made meaning that avert our natural inclination toward emotion as sensing abstraction: the language of feeling. Wholeness can have no need to focus on a single regard to Reason when Reason enters the collective emotional stores.

What is abstract has no biased meaning and thus no Blame. Feeling moves rapidly along the synapses to the brain's storage areas. Dispersed, each focused verbal tone is unified in sense.

The Provocation that stems from meaning, designed for function and for Reason, keeps us trapped in Blame Loop that is barren of Self-imaging by pure feeling reference. The simple partial fact that we disengage from natural sensing signals the warnings—the signals—that speak to us through our inwardly directed anxieties. No animal is gratified by life inside a cage.

Provoker Function provokes Blame. Blame provokes Impasse. Impasse is Paradox. Last Reason held and tolerance stretched for function is Blame Loop Synthesis—our ethical manifold of eternal infernal hope and bulwark of last gasp Reason for Reason sanctified—agreed, believed and utilized as Knowledge. Life itself is not the yield of Knowledge but is a never-ending study of quickly decaying facts and enacted Truths for which we will kill before we will abandon, though in time and by the capricious sanction of group, we will abandon all. How, then, shall we define madness?

Children play among skeletal ruins and we find Excuse. Children warm themselves beside garbage and we extol and glorify Blame in the name of God and savior and humanity. Dare we speak to such children of conscience? Do we tell them of our time-wrought consciousness and deliver for them our pale representation of green tree? The children are alive and full and complete. We are flat and comatose in the made world of our prejudices and jerry-built woes—our propped up sadnesses. There is no justification and no warranted, authorized excusable Blame to redeem us. None!

In Paradox, there exist overwhelming problems that cannot be solved with currently ensconced mind-set Reason; nor can they be "felt away" through arbitrary beliefs and lip service to Intention. Mothers and fathers of deceit must expect deceived children and that their children's children will also be deceived. For how long will we hide behind noun/verb protocol?

Man must break down and rejoin with that which is his inherent nature. If we cannot do this, then concrete, steel and technical consumption will destroy us even as we destroy ourselves. We will come to know what the children know: that our sacrifice of them to a symbolic Gehenna and Lake of Fire is the means to a thinkable end and a mental undoing.

Does such offered explanation sound negative? Is negativity offensive? Then we must consider what is negative and offensive by motive and coercion. Provoker Function is not real; nor is it concocted to represent what is real. Provoker Function is no more than language employed as fortification of single-minded end results that are maintained as a source of profit for the pompous elitist manufacturers of I-to-We incorporate thrust with authorized right, exclusive to hypocrisy. We abide by the law of the land and its dictates and adjutants. We console ourselves with Half Fact, Half Light, Half Real, Half Life becoming Half Truth as maudlin Truth for inhuman, uncivilized, hoaxed knowledge bent on generating gain for Future Promise. We abide within a halfhearted dream based on a surreal covenant for power and glory and wealth. We dwell within sad realms of perverse strategic advantage, willing to think that we "best" the other guy before he "bests" us. Merely business? War is a business and a profitable one. Starvation is a business—and murder and plague. We sing praises to a merciful God. What cunning hypocrisy! We have no mercy at all.

If none of this was so, human beings would know that Provoker Function could no longer exist as a prime good over evil nor as right over a contrived wrong. If none of this was so, partial fact would be engaged by Feeling to become whole fact and universal parallel of consciousness—beyond non-gender Self–interrogation, down into pure Feeling, transited with Reason. If none of this was so, human beings would bring to discipline one simple rule: Thought is doubt and it reaches deep into the synthetictic well-being that we denote as our civilized selves. If none of this was so, the human being would be acutely ashamed to profit from misery. If none of this was so, the human being would disobey the laws and rules that entrap and ensnare, and he would not commit to the memory of his past the names of things that inflict.

If we can deduce Reason and repair the severed sensual wholeness of being—Feeling to Reason and Reason to Feeling—The Creature will be given an elemental place for its work in perfect Now. Needs will then become basic mandates in a rational fact-to-fact study of Self and not before-the-fact preordination of right or good dependent upon a Blame Loop business of contention.

As long as we stand to allow ourselves the subtle measures of Provocation for function, knowingly sanctioned, and as long as we stand for Intended Reason, all that can be replicated and Dutifully justified will be replicated and justified. All that can be sanctified and sold will be. All that can be predestined and falsified by Impasse and Paradox will be. Reason will fail. Already, we enter Reason Fantastic, a sure sign that Reason does battle with the phantasms of religion for control of the minds of the minions, as the possibility of a Dark Age looms. Feeling will be witness to human, animal and environmental losses, but Feeling will not fail. A new and different kind of Gray Age will ensue.

Blame Loop Synthesis is forging alliances with psychological think-strategies and religious power-housing. As a unique specie, we can no longer afford these rituals nor any ideals that are laced with the further separation of instinctive sensing.

Before the last Dark Age, from 476 A.D. to 1000 A.D., philosophy, linked with art and literature, warned of impending danger. Certain renderings and literary articulations illustrated, through grotesque imaginings, that access to the mind had been closed off by belief and Reason Impasse. Want for stimulus became locked in Impasse. Want for stimulus was, for many wasted years, locked in immovable place for position and structure of power. Throughout history, as now, every synthetic group formed from Paradox seeks control over meaning—control over The Word: The Word turned God-Word and God-Word turned God-Meaning. If this sounds ridiculous, then what is more revealing than men or women who walk down a busy street closely inspecting their surroundings? What is more furtive and frightened than their hasty glances? When a specie bodily fears the members of its own specie at large, there is danger of annihilation.

In the last decade of the twentieth century, we do not have to look far and wide to see signs of decay. Those signs are as near as our own hearths. There is no philosophy. Literature and art have both been bought and sold—laid low as decadent presages of pure Reason in name only.

As we stand on the brink of a New Age of Darkness, we are girded with the strength of our own artifice. We are becoming more empowered and entitled with more and more fear drawing close. We are failsafed by loyalty to duty and provisioned and privileged as believers and shareholders within the Loop of Blame.

Humanity is deadlocked and Impasse is held. Urgency precludes art: No Dark Age comes without foreboding art—the heartache of wrenched feelings that churn. We need only witness what is already in motion. We know black and white realities well: Emotion is white heat.

Until all darkness has passed, art must disenchant itself from its detractors to assume a Godly role most humbly. Art is the voice of First Voice Incarnate. The more that Reason fails, the more that words disintegrate, strain and slip. Art illuminates anxiety. Art is a seer into the heart.

It has been said, "A fool sees not the same tree that a wise man sees." How have we been fooled?

Define green tree. What is Provoker Function?

NOTES

NAME: DATE:

NOTES

NAME: DATE:

V

V

BLAME LOOP SYNTHESIS

Agreement-Processed Noun/Verb Inversion

Mankind will not be reasoned out
of the feelings of humanity.

—Sir William Blackstone

IGNORANCE DOES NOT JUST CONSIST OF NOT KNOWING, nor is it an innocence of will. The inductive mind tags what is unknown with undue distinction and draws conclusion that mental description is made representative fact and an exponent of all that is deemed real. Made fact is imitation and replication pursuant to imagined logic. Made representative real is secondary Intention. What is inherently real is recorded by the passive sensual Self and held in Sixth Sense, *a priori* or first representation, neither real nor unreal.

Provoker Function assumes a role for invention of made-meant-to-be fact, portrays it through Reason, and represents it through Agreement Process that is designed for secondary act: Intention.

The Agreement Process is the method of imagination that knowledge presupposes ignorance through installation of clarified symbols in a labyrinth of flat-line labels controlled within an altered state. By controlling the labels of the mind, it is possible to control the mind.

This is the sub-parallel broken off from the senses. Symbols, not sensory stimulus, occupy active pursuits.

This is our feeling of incompleteness and this is our split in

Reason and emotion. This is Blame Loop Synthesis, for purpose remembered.

Provoker Function endows such symbolic memory with denoted underlying logic that fuses ersatz life to promised form. Truth is as Reason does in promised sub-parallel realm. We live in an altered state of promise with sense-altering symbols implanted for Intention—as Agreed—to produce circumstance.

Reason closely models passive memory, except that Reason is a timed contrivance and rigged in Future Past. But the mind can only hold portions that are made viable with fact Agreement and that must be constantly rehearsed, re-taught, and re-played to keep from being washed away as feeling, outside the residuals of vested time, devours all facets of active memory in Future Past.

Imagination reaches into the Reason parallel for commonly recognized think-process imperatives—to place them in active memory complete with social approval and disapproval. This right of conquest of Reason for Reason over recorded passive memory is not an inborn feature of the human creature. The right of conquest has been implanted and taught by construction of a Blame Loop Synthesis with made results that conclude Reason.

Blame is the logic that good and bad are each enemy of the other. Blame is the indifferent exchange of what is good that may become bad and of what is bad that may become good. Good and bad do not matter as long as Blame can encounter enough sentimental replicates of pre-thinking that it can be brandished in any direction that seems popular or accepted. Such rite of Duty for Blame, combined with the Agreement Process, creates a working synthesis for censure and impunity. Such logic is justification for Reason to be used. A circle has no end: Blame is infinitely reciprocal.

We live in manmade Paradox. Reason is Impasse. The Blame proponent is Reason manifest—Reciprocity in Paradox: R.I.P.

Blame Loop is a pre-conditioned made-meant-mean reality

that is authentic to Belief and that is validated by systematically drawn-off Reasons for method justification and resultant end think-processing: We have what we want always.

Blame Loop is service-oriented for jobs, position, empowerment and dependability upon results. Blame Loop in Entity is both a franchise of Progress and interlard of acquired time.

Fear of Blame inhibits exposure of even those things that are tolerable. Self-awareness is denied and opposed. Active memory fear of Blame directs the human being toward inhibition through knowledge. Knowledge is the manifest of subconsciously implemented fear. Innate sensual Fear is directly responsible for clarity of Reason Logic placed for Intent use in active memory. We cannot withdraw from our senses that wax and wane: There is no saving grace beyond the inward cry.

Knowledge is hypocrisy and it employs tacticians for service to any domineering thing that has not been declared fiction, for easy osmotic diffusion into Blame Loop. Active memory focus and use depends upon group charge for information to be used. One must be able to remember and to perform as expected, without question.

In introspection, we deduct and define until we can step out of the normal capacities of symbolic think-base to arrive on a collision course with substantial conscious pre-meant logic that is moved by Intent. All Intentions are shortly carried and end abruptly. Intentions waver beneath the illogic of Reason—its transient gains and losses. Passive memory tells with emotional drawing. We thrash around in the mental cradle until nothing more can be deduced except a primal scream.

The scream is the human being's first voice and first language. Within the womb, we are nurtured by that which is respectful of life, which is felt and which remains silent. Within the womb, there are no questions asked that cannot be answered with the sustenance of blood, carrier of life itself. In utero, we are not strangers to ourselves, and all that we think and feel is not adversary to Reason nor opponent to a silently resolute mind. We are unborn to rank and status and quick-fix place. We have not yet been born as a predator; not yet met our false gods nor fashioned Reason from Knowledge.

Birth begins our delivery into Blame Loop Synthesis. At birth, we know that fear can show us how limited we are in scope. But it is shortly after birth that we become immune to feeling generated, as if adaptation quickly utilizes a quiescent being. We are alone yet complete and unlimited in our equalizing specie drive, with its unquenchable thirst and appetite for life. Our senses can retrieve much more information than we can handle. It is the weight of remembered activity that hinders the mind's full use. As children, we see through Reason but learn to allow it. In youth, we remember to remember but have no memory of what is important to the essence of Self—such distinguishable highlights that outline surface realities as a magnetic signature that we etch deeply into the conceptual origins of our minds. We feel and feeling passes and we feel again. We adjust, not because of Reason, but to Self. The active mind, before filling, is a passive mind that neither seeks Intention nor Reasons for it. The human being is adjustable. Silently and surely, we feel.

There is a hold on humankind that causes us to measure and limit our scope of thought that cannot be measured and is an infinite to wholeness. We scratch at it and pick at it, stumble over it and remind ourselves of our humbleness. In our Reasonable chase after the infinite, Reason, the infant sojourner, has fallen. Fallen, the gentle Creature becomes The Beast. In our dismay at Reason failure, we chastise The Beast for failing to perform to the false standards of our implanted expectations— our whims within Duty, our performance-rated dogma, and our failure to arrive at some sort of sterility that will gain us admittance to a tiresome, mechanical world.

In our unease, we feign disregard for a feeling Beast or, through the tenets of civilization, we abuse The Creature that is Self. Reason was designed as antithesis for fear. Reason was to have been our failsafe and barrier for all time. Within the word-safe haven of Reason, programmed Reason could not fail.

In antiquity, did the Greeks sense the rush of emotional flooding as the signals of their downfall issued warning and as human conduct became such that any lesser animal would have deemed it imprudent and unwise by base instinct alone? Can we sense, in our midst, as most certainly did the Greeks, our mental undoing? Can we identify and mark this sub-parallel slit within the civilized mind?

Why is an infinite that is not part of Self-interrogative questioning that asks how, when, where and what. As inquiry, Why becomes a beleaguered and strained trick question that, in the pull-down of Reason to Reason, or in the upward thrust of Reason Stacking for Reason, is whetted as a dialectical sword for Intention. Noun/verb inquisition controls dualistic think-processing. At any place within this sharp vernacular contrivance, there may be inserted a logic, and it is such a mad logic that makes Why a divisible to infinity that can distract us and delude us with its minutiae of subterfuge and concealment. Remembrance of Why logic is the recitation of Blame doctrine or Reasoned Intention. *Why* is the annunciator of our straitened and sized schizothymia—the division of The R.I.P. in universal parallel. *Why* is a feint within a feint ad infinitum and the synthesizing and enveloping logic of Blame Loop. Impasse depends on institutional Paradox.

At first, entrance into Paradox is encouraged. Next, it is imposed. If necessary, it is enforced by code and law to insure obedience to premium beliefs that are set aside as conspicuous orders for logic. It is the heavy credence given to logic, by enactment of penalty and fine, that convinces us of its ubiquitous worth. Laws are piled upon laws until new jobs are needed to handle the overflow of newly made criminality. Profiteering from bad becomes good. Such inertia in the recognition of substitute Self-worth, and the all-too-willing giving over of the Self to a direct Entity, are left over from the days of the Mystics, who

could not transcend Reason spent as Knowledge for motive acti-
vated Reason and whose heresy became dogma. No systematic
linking of either heretical or orthodox chains of logic can long
reign over The Beast in its desire to know Self.

An abject implementation of over-riding Reason propels one
forward; the same contemptible logic becomes ward to all that
is made rational, overlapping sensual interrogation and pushes
out the natural Self. What is made rational is a want for what
works to remain workable and unchanged. Rationality, as made
to mean, keeps Blame Loop and the Infinitum of Why intact—
without break and with absolute law to be obeyed. This is last
reason held: the blind end of Impasse. Within Blame Loop,
there can be no diverting of mainstay cause-and-effect cir-
cuitous formula. The naturally rational Creature does not function under the influence of dual Reason except for Reason
enhancement and prototype.

We are made to respond; we must react to join process. Consciousness is formed from subconscious memory implants—the
symbolic language of words. Sound rules the mind, backed by
word-written proof. Religion claims the spoken word and politics claims the written word that becomes law.

When we look deeply into the eyes of religion, we do not see
an omnipotent God that is the remedy for the mandated fear
that controls man and woman. We see a semi-divine facsimile of
a God Entity that is a leech on the human mind. The parasitic
God of Doctrine sits upon a host of wadded bodies congregated
for supplication—each body, by bawdy Intention, contorted and
remade in hopeful supposition; each being implanted with synthetic fear that cannot be transited into parallel consciousness;
each adorned with the trinkets of word glory, garbed in robes
specked with the bony iconic shards of a splintered Self for
abjuration.

Stillborn of actual thought and barren of actual deed, we are
provoked for function into the logic of dispelling this unknown
fear for safer fear, controlled by men of Reason and consumed.

Our humanity is heaped upon the bulk condition of social morality. There is no greater Provoker Function than the religion of social dictates.

We destroy the very thing that we worship and sing praises to our share-held bloodsucking God of duty. Duty killed Christ.

That such a plundering thing as religion can be denoted the same as the Eyes Behind the Eyes and the Light Behind the Word that could be something like God is blasphemous to all that could be but is not Now. There is nothing to remember— no mystery, only feelings permeable—in the always-dissolving Now of Self. Ersatz Momentum forbids what could be Now, for Now does not favor Progress but does favor human concern for human concern.

Philosophy predicates an irresistible urge to favor feeling, but due to the plainness of such an inclination and the prissy need to present as a nobly intellectual discipline, it purposefully stands clear of the virtue of feeling. It always safely refers back to the last attempt at "through the looking glass" and goes no further. Philosophy speaks as though it has a fairy-tale fright of bogeymen and trolls! This is the reluctance to reconnoiter things which are abstract—kept behind Impasse and paradoxical formulae.

What is termed abstract is not abstract, but is the consequence of our inability to fully sense, decipher and deduce, whether it is the process of trying to discern a smell or to find a sliver of wood in one's finger or the abstraction of interpreting a new language.

Feeling is the first language in the First Voice of the human being. What may seem abstract is not abstract if we may learn to deduce it and to understand Sixth Sense Self-communication that is the emotional pathway and the mental bridge and sensual conduit to our living core of Self.

Human beings are sensually telepathic and, if the senses are in working order and attended, may reduce an entire active memory archive of alliterative metaphor to a soothing collection of passive data and sensual striae. The feeling, sensual being is not a Reason manifest carrier nor meant to be. The Creature longs to forget what it is required, by Reason, to store in memory.

Those who are in Reason service are conditioned to consider sensuality to be a disorder: One is said to be over-sensitive, over-sexed, over-emotional, over-compensating, over-indulgent ad nauseam. Through Reason, we are made liable to legal tender —duty sanctioned in station, position and fidelity to word disposition that is made-meant to mean and followed blindly. We succumb to duty for the reward of promised vainglorious image. Our God is our image of divine control, divine profit, divine time, and divine rote in duty.

Knowledge by rote for resultant end and Blame Loop production is the republic of bottom feeders who pursue human misery for consumption and who seek refuge in license. Bottom feeders peddle placation of misery for sorrow and mollification of fear at high premium for low return. Such low behavior that we attribute to crustaceans is our livelihood and our method of progress and timely duty. How do we differentiate survival from stealth and cunning? How do we differentiate will to survive from will to conquer and master? How do we define the treachery that spills from the horn of plenty?

Feeling is not a thing that is cloying, as are sincerity or heartfelt affection. Feeling is the most elemental moving away from deceit that is the Agreement Process.

If we willingly fail to feel, do we not also fail to think and fail to Reason? Feeling is aspiration to full faculty of life—to not arbitrarily believe Reason as justifier for destruction.

Do we succeed by division of the infinitum of Why? Can we measure our successes, particle by particle, like tiny grains of sand, counted and numbered by hand? Would it not be as wise for the blind to lead the blind? *Why* is the mastering governance of a master race, bled by Reason and for the failing of Reason. How arrogant are we to hope for the consecrated Why of tomorrow!

When we consider that caprice is permitted to Reason, we must also consider the method of caprice—the motive for sudden change of Reason for no Reason. Though caprice is often attributed to feeling, it belongs to Pretense Reason, Last Impasse and failsafe that becomes illogic. Feeling does not permit out-of-context acts, nor does it allow prefixed meaning. Now and transiting feeling blend as one. There is no R.I.P. in the constant of Now.

The being that is personified as one human individual is subconsciously made to react to manufactured implication and toxic method.

We loathe this. We sense it as slick on slick. It encumbers us and harms our completeness in first voice.

Few will admit this and fewer still will part from it to stand separate from Entity Logic. We subject ourselves to a method of caprice and look for synthetic Blame as Reason savior and as right over others who will not Agree to Agree.

The false parallel of word labyrinth and function mandate tells us what to say, how to act and what proper symbols to think-process. We are the puppets of our own despair and we drown in the sadness of our Reasons.

We are so desperate to know and to control that we disengage from the silent world of sensual grace to parrot empty verses from memory. We opt for a legacy of apostasy that abandons a fully dimensional Self and bonds us in Blame—at Impasse—in Paradox. The mask of willing hypocrisy will fit anyone who is willing to Agree.

It is within Blame Loop Synthesis that the I-We-They is born into Impasse. Each share-held function of license and legal right is at a formulated Impasse and in Blame Loop—jobs for jobs imposition.

Paradox and Blame comprise the Agreement Process and The R.I.P. in the human mind is widened. What does Blame Loop Synthesis enact?

NOTES

NAME: DATE:

NOTES

NAME: DATE:

VI

—————— VI ——————

CIVILIZED MAN

The Pretense with Which Man Chooses to Live

To see what is in front of one's nose
needs a constant struggle.

—George Orwell
In Front of Your Nose

NATURAL OR INBORN FEAR is the innate reluctance to interact with or continue in the line of or move in the direction of alarming impulse. Due consideration must be given to such threatening interference. To feel afraid commands our attention.

Early man, in his original Self-state as a so-called cave dweller, had no Reason—no future tense momentum toward progress and no made Intention. He passed the test of two hundred thousand years duration with nothing more than his innate drive for the satisfaction of his basic needs.

The caveman was a gentle creature. One hundred ninety thousand years of communal living prove his worth and stamina. That he never compromised or altered his state of existence attests to his vitality and his special integrity.

The original Self ancestor of the sapient modern man was uncivilized. We, within the tight security of made I-We-They massive movements for strategic disregard, stake ownership in civilization; so far have we progressed in our acquisition of knowledge and Reason Pretense. The original Self ancestor, who dwelled most uncivilly, without written words and without the construct of symbolic speech, in caves and jungles and forests, did not own nor want to own nor have a notion of owning. He was The Beast—the minotaur lowered into the labyrinth of proprietary promise.

Modern man owns dearly what he has made himself become: a hyper-civilized mechanical half-breed technological drone. Our humanity lost, we have become our own automatons, force-fed on implanted symbology and provoked function that yield, with the clarity of vacuity, still life future in a hole. We do not even come close to living. We project, and our haughty projections are more like thin and feeble patterns on a barren flat wall than like anything that could be the supple animal called human, whose muscle and bone moved by acts of his own volition. We act by dictate only. Modern civilized man is a graft bonded to a cybernetic cosmos by one pale fleshy thread and suspended in Supernature. Dangled thus, and hung, we are the master race of humankind undone for good and evil, with a mental crevice filled with the inversions of warrant and empowered offerings.

Such a creature of silence was our original Self ancestor that he knew his place and kept it. First Voice was complete and it spoke clearly through the physical language of sensual display and gesture. Fear, as he knew it, was not something that had to be manufactured. Fear was his friend and he walked its paths; respected it as a single sense, divisible to a whole. He had no smugness of good and evil; knew no morality of right and wrong. Sensual definition was his guide—his silent partner. He knew serenity and peace of mind. His sense of fear and his value of it signified his union with mind/body at work with nature, not against it.

Compare this serenity with the strain imposed on modern man in his quest to reach the pinnacle of such a thing as political correctness or religious right. Seen without method of Reason and Intention, such a planetary effort of clawing and tearing can be viewed clearly as the Self-annihilating activity of a specie tempered for destruction. Reciprocity in Paradox is final Reason empowered.

As each generation hands down its inventions and technological marvels, nothing changes except that our yen for our own extinction increases with each succeeding generation of humanity, grafted to cybernetics. We are half-bred into a symbolic life that speaks the gray and watery language of our invented gadgetry. Our close symbiotic relationship with machines has grown so that we have become mutated scions to a machine race and a machine legacy. What is machine-managed is time-exclusive and does not bear on well-being or the satisfaction of doing at a slower, unhurried pace.

Our slipshod attempt at language does not come close to touching those things that once were most pure within the transparent heart of the human essence: gentleness, affirmation, feeling and passive memory. These elements invoke doubt to thought. To remain whole, the human being must retain these as the inquisitors that can bring emotional joy.

The transparent heart has been replaced with Blame Loop. Blame Loop is a viable business based on what is and is not politically correct, when political correctness is, in partial fact, the most successful working con ever devised. Its scope is global and it permeates even the lowest rungs of modern society. However, in the age of cybernetics and latter-day R.I.P., it is considered antisocial and a mark of near criminality to speak of politics as anything other than the most forthright and legitimate service to humankind. One who is Self-educated beyond technology, and who persists in ignoring and maligning political credence, is criminal in thought, if not in deed, for he is out of line with societal Intention. Petty malefactors against the written law of Entity are encouraged to commit their petty felonies, and their crimes are condoned or pardoned. If common acts of thievery and murder were not condoned and honored, we would have no need of prisons. New laws make new criminals. Politics and law protect jobs and duty only. There is no protection and no guarantee for the recreant misanthrope who, within the context of Agreement, is anyone capable of original

unintended individual thought. Thought is the ultimate transgression against think-process. Thought, without Intention to
mitigate, mollify or placate, is the ultimate crime against Reason. To reason against Reason for Reason is unthinkable: It
holds all reward and right.

Civilized man does not think, nor does he have need to
think—such is his pre-thought right word aim strategy and
advantage. Aim and motive, as flat-line strategy for Reason Pretense, are airy functions that, intentionally, produce nothing
other than the hybrid of non-thought that passes as knowledge.
To know is to merely remember on cue. To know is to be
included and ranked according to what is made and intended
known and serviced to credited institutions of labeled learning.
Catchwords and buzz phrases abound in the world of latter-day
R.I.P. Virtue is gross information for Entity propagation and
well-being does not matter. Language skills and comportment
determine the levels of trusted expertise within political correctness. It is prudent to capitalize upon the weaknesses of the
human being in the name of education and in the name of
progress—in the name of God.

Words are made-meant to be obeyed, and the terminal meaning of all words is obedience. Doctrine substitutes for sensual
feeling, and it is the basic criteria from which we live or half-live
in insubstantial bits and pieces—in fallen frames from still-life
future in a hole. The master race, in Supernature, is the race of
the moribund undead in last Reason held and Impasse is the
present disregard. Servility becomes us.

Our mental constructs and psychic scaffolding are formed,
one by one, as reedy props for Reason until there stands a
lethal labyrinth of Reasons stacked for Reason, and Reasons are
stacked against an original thinker. The honey-coated promise
of Reason hangs from a sequence of false sufferings that contort the subconscious emotions of the original Self Beast that
belies our altered state. We know sadness, but even our sadness
is worthy only of billing and profit.

Original Self-sensation and response are muted while our voices of false guilt and made duty are buttressed by the structure of Entity. There is no shame in Entity as the entire planet suffers and misery goes on sale. We are rewarded for the motive of hate as we are rewarded for its alleged opposite, the motive of love. Both are blank indications of Entity obedience and exist for the same Reasons of still-life future surmise. Within the Blame Loop of Entity, we submit our emotions for an exchange of paper that is the modus operandi of the present disregard. The perfect hypocrisy is the perfect Agreement and mandatory correct role playing in word use.

Our senses are atrophied. We favor in-place and enforced sub-parallel that brings us altered state comfort but hangs us high, as pale instruments within the sterile synthetic colloid of Supernature. Through word inversion, we Agree to favor two senses while suppressing the summation of five.

We turn our freedoms over to mundane still-life results that are the properties of two sensory apertures half used as consigned by the voice of It. Our senses are ripped by the word. Sight and sound are made myopic, made tinny.

The R.I.P., as it widens to a breach, bleeds out feeling in a deep remorse that we fail to touch, for if we sensually realized it, Reason would falter and our slender, propped-up constructs would topple and fall through. Within the deep remorse of our failure, we neglect original Self and choose Paradox for its brittle word portrayals of glory and power and safety—one song of sadness for every will inverted. The word labyrinth grows and its vortex pulls until we can no longer recognize original Self, lost as we are in the maze of Reason made for Reason and Reason Behemoth. Illogic is the potential of logic.

As sensual myopes, we fall. Yet original Self is finite and resolute—not exclusive to Reason. Feeling is *a priori* cause and effect of the original Self though our every circumstance is planned in justification.

Base sincerity from Paradoxical Entity does not connote honesty from verbal taunting nor from the shorn integrity of original Self, but denotes I rebuke to prevent Self awareness. Provoked Intention precludes real momentum either toward the bait of consigned position in regulated comfort or away from it. We are damned if we do and damned if we do not, if not sanctioned.

Civilization is word-worthy syncretism and duty-bound hypocrisy with original Self-Feeling baying at its heels. Civilization is the attempt to squash the internal roar of emotion that is always in the way of Reason manifest. The hypocrisy of civilized duty is favor given for favor received. All is neat and proper until the reward system is tilted into enactment of a predestined Agreement Process that excludes anyone from entering without joining and becoming process. Unless one is authority, one has no authority. Robbed of authority and governance, even over Self, one is devoid of anything except sentiment: the sloughing off of hope—the faithfully faithless expended.

Legal ramifications are used by those who can affirm and deify sanctioned logic in strategic stance and argot use. Understanding is not wanted nor warranted. Compliance is required. The most word-servile enjoy full access to word labyrinth as exchanges are made, and oversee all lesser language use as sentimental diatribe that is without virtue and is not inclusive. Believers, as underlings, assume that current jargon is the last and final word and, therefore, first and only. They plummet, like racing lemmings, into an unknown sea and are submerged in mono-dimensional mind-set to bob and dunk for jobs, for jobs of labor offer nothing of substance that is produced for creative gain.

Altered mind-set favors documentation, warranty, exclusivity and empowerment and gives them gravity within the time distortions of progress. However, Impasse of the altered state is nothing more than mind-set in a sell-athon of promised failsafe for the hoax of moral and ethical contrivances—the long mental pins and braces stuck through to hold us in Paradox. The faux concrete base and weightiness of infinite Reason based on

Why is foreign and malignant to mind/body continuum and working feeling.

Viewed from our favored stance—within our super-civilized and hyper-sapient and method-organized time/place productive milieu—the lowly caveman seems uncouth and obnoxious—a creature prone to violence and bestial acts of savagery and ferocity. However, our modern and adroit wisdom veils, in Reason slick, the partial fact that these past two thousand years of justified civilization have killed and tortured enough of humanity to populate the entire earth, leaving not one square mile untouched by the animus of man.

What meaning do we give to civilization? How far do we carry such a label into Provoker Function? Give God to the savage and take his wealth? Whom and what do we tag and whom and what do we leave untagged? Within a made quagmire of meant words and proceeded meaning, when do we scrape our share of redeemable goods from the top and leave our children to scramble? When does madness become falling apart? When does Reason topple? What end do we seek while executing a sub-parallel altered state enactment that gives strange credence to forced mindlessness and made tasks for empty duty that cannot exist without an Agreed Blame Loop and Paradoxical failsafe to back it? Only in Agreement and by Agreement do we fail.

Within the doublespeak and doublethink of our barren civilized tongue, bad begets good until good is bad and a new symbolic good follows. This double-marshaling to order and method belies the swap—this building to symbolic upgrade only; this flip-flop of sanctioned right. Within double-culture, good and bad are precisely the same: for sale and profit. Only Reason is variable and interchangeable and slick. Reason designates what is good and evil. It is only through reciprocating opposition that we claim value and virtue. Beyond Reason, good and evil do not exist as virtue and non-virtue and are merely excuses to control and are our refusal to look into a finite Now.

We willfully refuse to see the misuse of children by religion, for religion is virtuous and controlled with symbolic fear. Yet we click our tongues and sigh over child abuse for the wrong Reason and blame those who do not believe.

We willfully fail to see the slaughter provoked by political right for right Reason; Blamable and contemptible. Yet, we click our tongues and sigh over the tragedies of mass murders that have, in latter day R.I.P., become commonplace.

We must ask: What is the difference between good and evil when they are, plainly, the same? What regulates murder and what condones petty crime? Can we say, with any certainty, that the taking of human lives is not sanctioned and regulated for Reason?

What of our cave-dwelling ancestors? Did they accomplish for Reason or for the satisfaction of some immediate and simple need? The human being, in an unaltered for Reason mental state, is in constant oneness with its first sensual language of emotion; it speaks in clearly reflected ordering of the senses, downward in scaled deduction to the point that, as sub-parallel is dependent upon the altered state of the verbal and written word, there are no words in an unaltered state.

Words, as footsteps, can be traced back to their source. They break down. They are shells whose contents must be emptied and used, the shells cast aside until they are dismissed and substance is revealed. If, as civilized and sapient beings, we cling to words and parrot them, verbatim, for display of knowledge, our words are hollow as we are hollow. We have nothing and we know nothing. It is merely the Intention to Agree and pretend.

Words are poor substitutes for the antediluvian, pre-civilized cry that requires no pretense and that holds no shame in its pure humanity. Without words, life is explicitly defined by interaction with the unknown in the parallel mind—not by provocation to memory.

The sub-parallel altered state controls human beings by forcing them to imagine realities that are far more seriously distorted than each previously imagined one as the walls of Reason grind and fall and we march toward Reason Absurdity.

We must realize that there is no Utopia, no Erewhon, no Eden that is beyond the Self. None. Variance has occurred, as foretold some two thousand years ago.

If we fail to register this warning, we will step back into a dark age where a handful of powerful people dictate rules and regulations for the many while the rules and regulations become more and more nonsense and the pitch of the voice of It rises to octaves that are painfully intolerable—a voice that is not only heard but is shattering and rending of our inborn ability to feel and to Reason, within the sensual order of Sixth Sense interrogation of Self. All that can be left from that are the rudiments of hate and destruction.

Blame Loop dictates mindless adaptation. It is Reason for Reason and it produces stamped out "cookie cutter" people in pursuit of Paradoxical stamped-out rewards. When can enough ever be enough when we are already running on empty into a void—when every gain is a loss and every loss is a falling apart? In falling apart, history shows that, pitted one against the other through legal engineering, we will gladly murder for Reason, steal for Reason, take sides for Reason, justify apartheid and engage in inquisition by bludgeoning. Within Blame Loop, decree of power is often want to kill.

Sometimes, if one whose humanity is intact does not pay correct homage to the group allegiance, the mental window of the Self is smashed. One becomes disheartened and angry; turns inward and doubts in a way that causes the wearing down of Self reliance. The being is lost and feels betrayed and often turns to psychology as the last possible savior. Psychology reinforces and implements correct thinking as a method of learned and prelearned strategy. Psychology is a manipulator for sanction.

Those who are diagnosed ill may either learn to play an obvious patient role by receiving drugs and prescribed therapy; or they may fall further back into the shelter of Self-doubt to the point that they are chronically disordered or labeled dysfunctional. In either case, the human essence is finally broken and the clear light of it is blocked out that would, otherwise, shine through as purity of insight and Reason, sensually tempered and experienced.

There is no need to ask why people commit suicide or harm others. Such provoked mechanisms of hostility are built into the system of knowledge. I-We become They. Society lives by and for symbolic fear.

Suicide, murder, insanity, thievery, indolence, ignorance, racial hatred on all sides, drug addiction and selling are condoned and encouraged. An industry thrives: Human despair is a precious gem. Its buying and selling has given us our complete ownership of modern civilized man, master and slave.

NOTES

NAME: DATE:

VII

—————— VII ——————

TRUTH AS *WE* KNOW IT

Half Life: The Promise and the Duty

If God did not exist, it would
become necessary to invent him.

—Voltaire

Truth is an artifact. Truth is made loyalty to a predisposed duty and it is duty to resultant end prophecy—a strident and rigged ideal. It is Truth As We Know It: a set of circumstances in which we believe in order to signify made Truth, contained as we are within a bloodless and wordy realm of emblematic labyrinthine mono-dimensional flat-line refuse in still life for falsity. We arrogantly believe all our controlled acts to be singular acts of volition, when volition is a legacy from our original Self ancestry that did not survive our rise from barbarity to civilization. By forfeiting The Beast, we forfeited free will. The human being gave up its freedom of movement for secured place in commanded culture: We own, therefore we succumb.

We pay only meek homage to bitter Truth when the duty of Truth is a sugar-coated placation and a cunning lure to Impasse Reason and Present Disregard. In disregard, we Agree. In Agreement, the human being fails completely.

All groups are dangerous because group mind is volitive, while original thought is prohibitive. Group volition sets artificial Truths through cohesiveness. To say, "We think, therefore we are," is group process-think. Political and religious right are based on such Truth: To think is to Agree. The sanctimony of state- and church-approved marriage is part of the large mock-Truth that uses group mind. It falsifies a state of false security for which we settle as love and which we think-process as love.

What is security but a falsified-for-Truth prevarication? When does love become dependence? When life itself is temporal, how can there be such a thing as a permanent secured Truth except as promised by group manifest? We force things to mean, when by the wearing away of natural passage, all things dwindle and fade.

Truth As We Know It is a planned ideal, pre-thought and fulfilled, so that we may say that we know all that could be kept and placed within a dimensional Sixth Sense sphere, maintained and gently governed by a five-feeling matrix of sensory Self-awareness: To say, "I see, hear, taste, touch and smell, therefore I live," recognizes all things held in memory for active service. What finer ignition to full life than the robust combustion, fueled by the audacity to disagree with suspect momentum of still life, held at Impasse in memory to rule only remembered enactment!

The main humanistic drive to whole life is resolute feeling. Drawn out through introspection, sensorial feeling yields the strongest foundations of art, its crafting squeezed out from pen and pencil, until feeling becomes form within the boundaries of creation—until art is synonymously picturesque of the human Essence. Composed from exquisite feeling, art and literature are two parts of the multidimensional sensual sphere which can enable the human being to connect surreal or ethereal imagination with Reason—through reverse ordering of sensual capacity, to retreat and inspect. Within such a sphere, the senses can overlap and combine to produce an outpouring of sensory Self awareness.

There is no one faction or group that can be blamed for the rolling force gathered in token Truth that has been witness to slow growth over the past two thousand years, with marked acceleration over the past two hundred and fifty years. The concept of Truth has helped to bring us to the dullness that we Agree to live as still life or an altered state of disregard—to an entire working, grinding, gnashing machine world of Reason designed and held as ersatz Truth. Philosophy has been traded for psychology and its resultant end strategic advantage. Psychology is, first, a business and a failsafe to Reason imposition that promotes disregard of the sensual animal nature of the human being while taking the specie ever further from its original Self-essence. Indeed, psychology has become so predominate within the patterns of business that merit is based on behavior. Such desperation to cling to a narrow definition of authorized Reason should warn us of impending danger.

We signifies a conversion of the human senses into side realms of mono-dimensional hazing. The human being becomes so devoted to the business of things and to the stilted language of doing for not having to do that he quite severs himself to a point that is quite removed from his original Self-nature and that only vaguely resembles the animal creature called human.

Essentially, the human being has made himself an artifact. It has been said that "We are symbols and inhabit symbols." Truth As We Know It is an artifactual symbol made-meant to mean absolute conformity to an Agreed ideal. Truth As We Know It is subject to schematic and arbitrary change, and human worth is measured by adherence to its Reasoned caprice. Truth and worth are our archetypal guidons; our paradigm; our emblematic Reason for joining Paradox. Those who manage to retain any traits of individuality are those who have learned to live by their wits alone outside of Agreement—on the fringes of symbolic circumscribing Intent. Such Self-reliance is becoming more and more a considered form of heresy to Truth As We Know It. In warranted Truth, the living human being will be smashed.

We find ourselves face-to-face with suspect momentum regardless of our convenient disregard. Momentum can be denoted as impetus or connoted as *a priori* charge for Reasoned effect of the infinitum of Why—the trick question never asked of Self but used on others as prevailing suction into Reason for reason—into the maze of disfigured word charged for functional enactment.

The natural senses of the human being are adjustable and Self-aligning. Each sense is restricted to its inherent boundaries: Sight is confined to vision and does not enter the realm of sound, nor does it use any language but that which is visual. Through the mind's sensual referencing, however, by overlapping sensual signatures of hearing, sight, taste, smell and touch, there is a multidimensional confluent stimulus that surpasses all mentally adapted singular codes and implants and goes directly to the heart of the human being. Sixth Sense bathes The Creature in a stream of unbroken consciousness of being complete and without need to separate one physical function from another. This convergence is constant to feeling and constant to Now; which was in existence before all intention. Without our markings, the convergence of the senses could be a taste of an ultimate Truth that is beyond our capacity to know. In this manner, it follows that all Truths are fallacies and all deemed positives are negatives. There can exist no right or wrong; no good and bad; for within the original Self-emotional corridors, we are beyond such makeshift jargon that is made-meant to mean for Reason.

All noun/verb lexicon is Reasoned Pretense or slanted to societal or cultural momentum. Thus, what is called expression is actually designed Intention. Within our altered state, it could be said that no communication of Self is possible unless the senses are stimulated directly and entirely—not symbolically. This refers to the kind of careful slowness that the civilized human being no longer knows. Speed and transitory flashes of light keep the civilized being's senses off track. Sleep becomes terrifying as the natural mind, below The R.I.P., runs against Ersatz Momentum.

Expression by labels and symbols yields action, but this is action that is accomplished by learned directives rather than

through a natural process of interrogation and creation. Noun/
verb criteria synthesize written and verbal momentum by insist-
ing upon Intent that can be easily judged to be accepted good
or bad or accepted right or wrong. When things are labeled
incorrect or bad, this indicates that Momentum is being altered.
This is Reasoned slick by trade, and those who seek to live up to
a role within Entity alter their behavior and mode of jargon
accordingly. Words in Paradox have no meaning. They are
badges of conformity.

Non-symbolic deductive thought halts active memory and
slows processed momentum until all doubt is removed. Doubt is
thought until the mind feels that it is no longer necessary to
doubt; that resolve has been reached through negative reciprocation. Thought is neutralized either by distorting and dissipat-
ing it or by dissolving it with whole sensual feeling. If thought is
felt throughout the informational bounty of the mind, Sixth
Sense receives it and matches impetus and symbolic carriage to
eliminate its return to doubt. In First Voice, we are naturally
deductive Creatures.

This let-down of Reason is the release of active memory
pursuits. Learning is by trial and error. Experience is by
reuse. We label the things that relate to feeling but are given
back to the intellect of the being as fullness of form and function interrogation.

Fear is always misunderstood; considered a culprit or a mon-
strosity. We are taught fear of fear that is our need for security—power in number mental meshing. Yet fear is our friend.
Fear says, "Test the waters and be careful." Profound inner messages come through loud and clear when adrenergic fluid is
pumping and the mind/body are one in recoil with sensual
awareness.

Fear is interrogative of unconcern that advances as right and
Truth and good. As long as someone can profit from the
moral/ethical/belief trinity, The Beast that is the disturbed
human Creature will not rest.

What is called the psychological side of the human personality is dislocated sub-parallel that is given symbolic preference and maintenance—sanctified active memory implants that are for reuse and profit. Psychological symbols are applied to all that is labeled dysfunctional and that inhibits Intention and pretense, for expert remedies and qualified programming—that is, the job.

Before the fact of Now constant, psychological dysfunction does not exist except through the empowered state of Impasse— the fabrication of We Entity and Truth portent. Is The Creature sick, or is it our Reason that creates mayhem justified by jobs? Psycho-systems are allied with Reason for Reason advocacy—the long gaping wound of The R.I.P—torn by what could easily be but that is not. The human consciousness could be completely healed if not concerned with the tug between the complacence of processed versions of good and bad; sped, with momentum, into Future Past, the fable of promise for Reason. We live in a history of discarded future hope.

Denying the sale of Self cushions our way into misery. We are taught much and it has no substance. Our character roles in jobs and in stratified status mollify our fear. Daily play-acts in jobs evaporate ideals. Self facade flimsily covers the hollowness that we sense, beneath all hypocrisy, to the fallen Self, a frail being that lies fallow—untouched, unborn and wasted. This wound in the Essence fabric marks our dedication to the imitation of life; our settlement for less when there is plenty; our willingness to succumb and be counted; our servility to Ersatz Momentum. Our hatred of it is hypocrisy. We allow it and we allow it to the letter of the law: Allowance is sanction.

The hoaxed charge of life imitation assumes disregard of Self and feeling and favor of Agreement, for Agreement precludes the knowing of Self. Reason is excuse. The Loop of Blame holds us, and right is given to those certified in power. Empowerment is the goal of the weak in mind.

Reason for Reason yields Reason. To continue it, we give it

status and meaning named Progress. To simulate motion, we reside in time. Future is the slant in time wrought from the promise of moving, and our loyal duty to think-factory will attest to the movement. This is a verisimilitude: the expectation of Truth when Truth is made.

When we are introduced, in think-factory and perfect Paradox, to share-held privilege, we are granted authority and license to blame, using it to justify position, status and longevity of resultant end cause and effect. I to We is a moving promise. We are locked into think-process that is slanted directly, by time, into Paradox.

The only way to realize the falsity of this state is to affect the momentum of verbal and written lexicon, Entity vehicle. All that is made-meant to mean is attitude loading. The achievement of higher learning is the achievement of a state that specifies authority with the jargon of canons and *corpus juris* devise. One can have a handsome stake in Paradox by remembering and responding to implanted cues. In this way, we can perpetuate the long-standing tradition of plundering a feeble and gullible society built on the artifact of Truth that is conditioned by plans of easy payment. The fallacy of We, The Truth, is tolerances that are falsified to run on empty.

Our parody of life is obvious. Paradox is hidden well behind the vested hypocritical belief in the transmutating, emulsifying, contorting business of religion that strips the human being of his dignity with its craftily choreographed rituals before a long-dead and superstitious God. If God was not dead, mankind would find it necessary to kill him.

Paradox is hidden well in our group adhesion for political awareness—our want to achieve, in capital progress, a safety-in-numbers reason for annihilation that favors Entity over Self. Everyone can subscribe equally to a promise of wealth in numbers . This is a kind of mental laziness and servility. As individuals, we take no risks and live in safe fear to rally for the good guy whom we appoint and who is poised to take credit for the demise, by any means necessary, of all opposition that is not dedicated to the sacrificial We. The unborn Self is immolated as part and parcel of altered mind-set to the drab life of original R.I.P. in Paradox. Beyond doubt, seriously applied, We status is protected with slogans and jargon that are symbolic failsafe against both feeling and interrogative Reason; dismissed as mere human wants and needs and, therefore, expendable, by inversion, before the monoliths of Progressive civilization and forward culture.

All sub-level transverse standards are provisional. All must admonish what is, at any moment, an object of hate in order to use and further the Agreement Process. For humankind to be worthy of respect without capitulation to the rule of word would blatantly point out misuse of Blame. Without Blame, Reason could not stand. Stripped of Reason, all symbolic ritual could be seen as perversion. Stripped of Reason, the one-act play of Truth, shorn of its facade of virtue for God, could be seen as an instrument of control.

Can the human being ever tire of its service to rule? Will he ever tire of playing the part of the arrogant slave, filled with venomous and bitter complaint, yet willingly bridled to its master? Given over to Reason, we are both master and slave, and the cycle of mock Truth in Blame will not be broken until Reason, as deceiver in imitation of life, is exposed as an antiquated method of destruction and its deadliness is finally annulled.

The stillborn in Reason essence of the human being is a Creature prone to forgetfulness, its supremely gentle nature unsurpassed by any other living thing; its sensuality evidenced by the delicate complications of its neural pathways; its strengths that are unfaltering, though not unyielding; its dire need to touch and to know beyond all

Our original Self ancestor, the intrepid cave dweller, certainly knew, despite its harshness, the splendors of life in the mind. In one hundred ninety thousand years, he was not relegated nor regulated, nor did he amass Reason. In his unaltered state, he made the splendors of the mind his daily choice. He had no need to understand momentum for Reason. His sensorial calm was his selection. He understood silence. Modern man, in his dominion of noise, places himself under despicable duress at breakneck speed. Another fifty years of such momentum will be disastrous. We are consumptive doers. One thousand years more of consumptive doing will bring a flight of despair so irreversible that the only savior will be annihilation from absolute misery that has become life: Self determined Apocalypse.

Negative statements are termed negative because they are not wanted. Negativity is dismissed because it is too serious, as though there could be such a thing as too serious consideration when we are Self-murdering.

Conversely, a positive statement could say, "There is no such thing as Paradox and no Impasse. We all want the right thing and the best thing, so everyone will Agree to do his part to help."

So, does Intent really matter or is it imposed, positive or negative? If all that we have is an Agreement Process, with a Reason for a Reason that instates and relegates to locked positions and roles, the business of portent is still suited only to resultant end. Words may intend the most positively virtuous right but if nothing is delivered but profit from misery, right, despite its positive Intention, is a raw deal.

Thought, in latter day R.I.P., does not exist. Without thought, positive and negative intent do not matter. The promise of Intent for virtue is profit from human strife.

There are erroneous terms well suited to the propagation of future tense coercion. One can be a good guy only by using good lexicon for strategic advantage for achieving goodness.

Correctness is rewarded. Belief, when Agreed, is always correct and certified by group license only. Belief in the pronoun I is pointless: It yields nothing. The group, en masse, is charged with right-think vigilance to insure the execution of rightful Blame. The group serves no other immediate cause and adorns itself with the profitable vestiges of Truth As We Know It. Duty and servility to duty come with a belief package intact—with ready-made symbology and onus, pre-thought and abridged .

Duty is made mandatory by sanctioned empowerment, contract and authorized prehension, with doctrine and law in generation. The artful manufacture of right and good is a business that produces misery for profit. The R.I.P. is a cash crop for those afraid of being afraid to think.

Duty, by strategic advantage, is the dictum of Truth As We Know It. Truth is the business of thought production in predestined Paradox for the Intentional building of Impasse, the last place that man can reside in active memory pursuit of Reasons stacked. Blame Loop is failsafed by moral and political facades that belie a sub-parallel, tenuously held by an Agreement Process, whereby the human being dangles over the yawning hole of The R.I.P., a breach in the human parallel of consciousness of life and the mental undoing of a species of Creature that is both inherently benevolent and, overtly, as haughty and proud as any bought slave.

The Agreement of the human being in R.I.P. is destined to fail, and it will fail in chaos, Paradox mayhem and Reason amok—in white godhead vengeance—until, laid low by gadgetry in androidal Half Life in Supernature, we crawl into the gray age of cyber-psychosis, discharged for Reason into Medieval Future Retold.

NOTES

NAME: DATE:

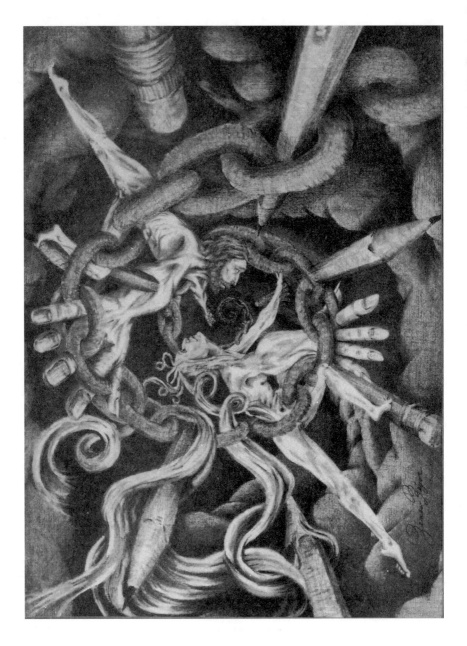

VIII

VIII

THROUGH THE LABYRINTH TO THE INVISIBLE SELF

Word Promise in Future Tense

We have our honey and the bee is kept so busy
producing it has no time to think
and make itself happy.

—From Hokku LXXI
Orientations of Ho-Hen, T. K. Hedrick

Entering the labyrinth of sub-parallel lexicon, we are compelled to satisfy Intention: such altered state of mind that exacts surcharge in the form of aphorism or strictly modeled maxim for use. It is the charge of lexicon to produce a forward of Now place that requites the senses to subservience for function with future promise of position. Position is the award for Entity certification to do. We attempt to do what cannot be done and, in so doing and undoing, mimic and mime from conscripted roles. The affect is one of simulation, a kind of shadow play of marionettes. It is a life that is not living and does not breathe except by use of established do's and do nots, the heroic codes that preserve Half Life made manifest by sub-parallel abstraction and word manipulation.

No language, in either written or verbal form, can express the sense of Self in a Now state. To say that only emotion does this or that only feeling can express it, after all interrogation has dissipated, sets the residual impulses of mind beside the residual impulses of body for the realization of place.

Sense of place, in mind/body continuum, educes a multifaceted and fully dimensional composite of Self that is beyond the proposition of made image. The polymorphic Self, as regulated by place, is nonjudgmental and relinquishes capacity for Blame. The polymorphic Self, in place, is free of The Agreement Process that governs the momentum of succeeding rules that implement future tense beliefs that disallow transition out of sub-parallel device.

Impasse/Paradox, as an occupied state of mind, renders the human being inert without mechanical means to propel it. The mechanics of Impasse move us to action through the mind-string puppetry of lexicon as warranted and charged. It is this shadowed mimicry of We Entity performance for I Place that grants illusory credence of I Purpose, based on ability to produce *a priori* results for results. Job ideation suggests future promise for future gain and Future redemption in I Place that is ahead of Now perfection. All that one must do is hold memory and Reason fixed to serviced Entity charge.

The mind, conjoined with the senses, is a computer or assimilator par excellence. There has been no machine invented that can realize or know or do; differentiate, identify, define and feel; such abstract information that comes before it. The human mind is a clearinghouse of proportions, scales and dynamic material to be evaluated. The largest share of interrogation is accomplished without the conscious focus of the being. Most deductions are automatic or so nearly automatic that full attention of the being is not needed. However, if attentive focus is directed explicitly toward the purpose of realizing feeling, the senses become inquisitors of Intention as motive and direct the Self inward, away from Reason for Reason and the hardness of an inherited made-meant-mean word, set aside from all applicable interrogative sense.

The word labyrinth is a mutated state of mind that reflects synthetic cause from effected appointment and splits the human being into two severed halves, one half being the facade that we present in memory. The other half is the domain of fear. It is fear of fear that keeps us in Half Life. It is what we willfully refuse to know that subdues us and traps us within the barriers of The R.I.P., breach in the Universal Parallel of Consciousness. It is the split of Reason and feeling, the split of the known and unknown, and the promise of tomorrow traded for redemption Now.

When we look closely into the eye of Entity, we see that its altered state is Agreed and that it is accepted but that it is never understood. We can conceive a good idea theory that, somewhere in space and time, we may be delivered to a doubt-free harmony, but we have no sense of the problem that is delivered from Paradox. We assume trust in things and situations that are distant to us and alien to our nature; words are mutations. We voluntarily enter into a labyrinth that has been structured from what we Agree to do in order to reap the rewards of a system that is designed to supply a synthetic and foreign human order that is manufactured for serviceable jobs and enough resultant end want to maintain momentum and I Place.

At what precise point is the human race in its acquisition of the labyrinth of sub-parallel lexicon? I/We Entity is degenerating. The Agreement Process is failing—not that individual human beings overtly desire to fail or consciously enter Agreement to fail as though participating in some massive Homo sapient suicide pact. Nevertheless, the good idea is redeemed as a collapsed and empty remnant of our once grandiose hope for tomorrow promise in future bright. We fail as we are made to remember to fail. We fail as we are meant to fail, and we fail as we mean and as we intend for Reason—within the tight bloat of our own constricted volition and acts of false free will.

Are we free by Agreement? We have no record that proves it. In the modern age of technology and a bridled proletarian science, we no longer have chariots to ride, for the chariots ride us. We deny ourselves our God of light and settle into religion as moral tyrant in wait for the fall of man.

In plain terms, God may be dead but not dead enough. The presence of God lingers still in the mind of the common man. Science and knowledge, as the arch nemeses of religion, have stuck hypothetical thorns in the hypothetical sides of God, in one form or another, for eons, and to no avail.

Ultimate control of the sapient specie has been up for grabs ever since human beings learned to speak and write—not before that. Before building his sub-parallel lexicon, man could have chosen to forsake his aberrant need to control and to be controlled, but he chose not to forsake and he placed himself on this earth as both master and slave.

Sub-parallel became quite strong in Celtic tribes during 2500 B.C. and became predominate during the Egyptian and Latin/ Greek periods, around 1500 B.C. Prior to this expansive blossoming of lexicon, Sanskrit and Vedic writings, as well as hieroglyphics, gave only vague history of what humankind was confronting emotionally. Very early on, the feeling nature of man was decried and abhorred. The Beast became a thing of shame and degradation. We hid our true nature in the shadow of our fear.

One need to only read a definition of the word "beast" in a modern dictionary to understand the evolution of that fear. To Beast, we attribute all surliness and malignancy. Beast is the marked receiver of all Blame Synthesis. Yet had humankind chosen the way of Beast, where would be our strife and where would be our pain? No sapient and wise Self-adoring Beast could morally construct of hydrogen atoms that which we, with Reason undone for Reason, have manufactured for profit and damnation. Beast, unlike The Retrograde, is neither master nor slave; it is fundamentally introspective and supremely caring.

God developed from Reason is an assigned caretaker of symbolic fear. If we fear Hell, then we must disdain God, so we worship in dread and worship the very thing that we abhor. There is no Hell in the human Beast—the very Self that we seek to control by the vapid and holy God of religion.

As studies of the development of Indo-European languages tell us, communication did not at first address differences in gender, as signification of gender did not matter. The original cry was more emotional than subjected to the purpose of sub-parallel charge. Future tense was not a matter for consideration. Future, in the mind, did not exist. Not until human beings developed a love of motion and speed did we come to require portentous promise for deed, which is duty as proscribed by guilt and duty as parodied by sin—the refusal to comply. Before humankind became focused on momentum and speed, sin and guilt did not matter. There was no need: There was no profit.

In early formation of language, single words or short statements were used. What was at first known as inflection became dialectic change. In time, as words were invented and pronounced more and more, vowels became singularly stressed and word endings regressed. A dialectical change occurred when case and gender made the transition from directives to functional nouns. Prior to this "-as" was masculine in gender while "-a" was feminine and "-u" neuter. Later "-as" was changed to "-es" so that vowels made all nouns plural regardless of gender or case. Restrictions were placed on words for obvious strength and command. Before this enhancement of language for the building of lexicon, mental muscle was only directly employed as strategic back-up for armies or group powerhousing. The elite moneyed class, who sponsored both word power and word command resources, held advantage over those less moneyed, who neither knew nor suspected that verbal/written word sub-parallel lexicon would transform the entire cubicle of world history into a networking of Agreements that demanded response. The manifest of lexicon became the destiny of mankind. Future inverted Now, and the momentum of man's life was assigned to it. Life in future promoted a regimented duty with extensive propping of false moral standard. People complied with this and were expected to comply with this as sub-parallel lexicon was passed from generation to generation until we came to what we have now: a hybrid phylum of human being that is degenerate—as foreign to its own original nature as it is to the original nature of its environs. Homo sapiens, indeed! Our wisdom is our grand conceit and downfall. It is the essence of our humanity that quakes and trembles in the presence of our made Selves; that is an I-We-They parody.

During the first centuries of word formation, man sought after comparisons of things and the exchange of information. His travels around the world and the slow pace he kept served as both an entertainment and a learning experience. Utterances were contrived as convenient ways of conveying common concerns and were not initially used as links to religious and political Entities. Later, extracted meanings were shifted and changed, by noun and verb pretense, into new-found express datum or command. With this sort of lexicon, man found that he could set the mental scene with vain messages of things to come. Agreement and reciprocal charge could be easily formed and obeyed.

The labyrinth that we enter through sub-parallel lexicon has but one entrance and no exit. If one is knowledgeable, then one has a map to the maze. If one does not possess knowledge, then one flounders in and around endless passages and tangles performing arduous tasks for Reason, quite aloof from Self. Through the mazes and knots within a mental jungle, the distance traveled is in direct visceral response to word messengers that have been learned by rote as key elements to sets of Provoker Function. Provoker Function propels us and Blame Loop Synthesis is our guide. Through Provocation and Blame, webbed and entangled until all feeling of Self is obscured, we are aware of only the clear wishes of Entity. We hear and accommodate The Voice of It. Within the labyrinth, we justify our contortions of Self for Reason. Homo sapiens has no other God than that which he has invented as master and slave. Outside labyrinth, we are not on this earth to struggle and toil not to kill and be killed. Our world is alive and bountiful. We abandon it.

Loyalty to sub-parallel lexicon and subsequent made thought is measured in terms of intellectual prowess and superiority. One is considered illogical or eccentric for relinquishing a share in this powerful symbolic network that holds both political and religious Impasse. Both are failsafe to any possible entry and exit out of the maze. The failsafe of religion is blind faith and trust, while the full share of Entity implies empowerment with status, wealth and validated I promise. One does not merely pass through the labyrinth but seeks the center. We, as standard-bearer for I principle, becomes the final base promise for future holding and noun place status to conjoin those within the league of sub-parallel lexicon in mutual Agreement and condescension to those outside the center of Paradox.

Through the labyrinth is a complete transition from The Agreement Process into clarity through the reassembling of the senses. Such clarification of the use of the senses realizes and directs ordering of Blame Loop/Provoker Function throughout all potential affects, so that the entire language of sub-parallel Entity is reduced to a few plain and simple axioms that can be easily used to favor a fortified Self that is capable of constant feeling to Reason convergence. Introspection, deduction and feeling become one. The R.I.P., then, can mend, and man and woman can continue their emotional journey to completion—to zero space and the perfect void.

NOTES

NAME: DATE:

NOTES

NAME: DATE:

IX

IX

LIFE IN THE MIDDLE

Eyes Behind the Eyes: The Senses

We must, however, acknowledge as it seems to me,
that man with all his noble qualities
still bears in his bodily frame
the indelible stamp of his lowly origin.

—Charles Darwin

THE ASCENT OF THE HUMAN ESSENCE from dormant Half Life Reason into the surfacing of mind/body feeling and its wealth may be called the Middle.

The internal mental matrix of the human being has not changed appreciably for two hundred thousand years. Biologically, we have adjusted to a shedding process that is no different from a goose readying for winter with an underlay of down which he then sheds for the summer. There is no point in trying to discover exactly why nature does this nor should there be a point to it.

However, the business of science is a profitable one that uses precisely such points of information to its advantage while professing pure concern for social good and correct observation with one or two twinges of ethical overtones. As long as any systems-think profiteering exists, Entity grows fat and placid with the arrogance of its Agreement and wise use of sub-parallel.

In light of this profiteering for good and true Reason in the name of science or machine or politics, the commonly accepted goals of goodness and truth must be dismissed in order to contribute to the plain definition of well-being. Used here, well-being describes the decency of Self-respect through non-use of the sub-parallel and its lexicon as hype-masters of fear, nor use of Blame for advantage and profit.

Through Impassionment, we may enter the labyrinth of sub-parallel lexicon; and understand it to the degree that it can no longer split off the legitimate feeling of the living senses of the human being. Impassioned thinking is the ability to feel and transit the explicit nature of a situation, Reason with it, and align it to a universal parallel of consciousness that is conducive to resolve through doubt.

Life in the Middle might be compared to the collective mind-set of the peoples of India. Even with obvious confusion from acquaintance with a thousand gods, and with progress nipping at their heels, they defer becoming victims of the real and live inside their minds. Their gods are imaginary and offer no redemption other than the reinforcement of the conviction that Paradox will not happen as long as Impasse is refused as a state of mind and as long as progress cannot consume them. Within the pleasantness of this simple conviction, these people have been able to enjoy, uncluttered by sub-parallel, active mind pursuits even as the glow of human essence is obvious and Self-respect is obvious; even when they are somewhat forced into ownership over their own impassioned objections.

Only civilized first-world nations exist in and for the sub-parallel of lexicon and use word labyrinth as strategic advantage. It is said commonly that "ignorance is no excuse."

Must one have an excuse in order to be fully alive? Is there a license of excuse to be obtained that says that it is all right with the political state for one to know and enjoy a rare thing of distinction? What are the demarcations of joy? Where are the boundaries of beauty and the parameters of ecstasy?

Using knowledge recklessly and with mindless disregard is ignorance, and there is no excuse for it except license.

The word labyrinth is slick on slick, and it changes like a chameleon: by quick irresolution or by flip-flop belief. Vigilance is required to keep up. It forces upon the human being excuse in the form of higher education for higher stakes in the race for material gain and status. The acceptance of this, by Agreement, renders ultimate excuse for ignorance as a most copious hypocrisy. Within this Agreement, the ends do justify the means, and nearly any abundance of ignorance is accepted as long as one meets criteria based on sub-parallel process-think achieved by adequately parroting certain bywords and phrases and maintaining a certain posture or stance. The best actors receive accolades and advancements. Skill is secondary. Intelligence, the Creature, is an emotional misfit.

The unfortunate part of this hiatus in the human consciousness is that there is no excuse for not knowing the existence of Paradox. We can deny Impasse based on a willing full-blown ignorance that is a halcyon disregard. By looking at upper-level users of the word labyrinth, the typical aggressive underling seeks a life at the top.

There is no life at the top. Life at the top is an illusion set upon mutual Agreement and resultant consequences that produce more and more Agreement for more and more consequences.

Unlike the Indians, whose culture rejects Paradox as excuse for life, the life in the middle of the civilized man is life in the middle of a split Self. The split Self does not carry the being essence obviously, with feeling and non-symbolic wisdom that can speak to the center Self with full sensual interrogation.

The middle life, as we know it, appeals to one maximally used sense. If the fancy is art, literature, music, dance or culinary delights, it yields single-sense middle life personification. We hold to the vacuous truth that the split Self can summon the imagination to produce art. Imagination, at most, is a side effect of creation which is a "busy hands are happy hands" means of entertaining the I-We-They circle of prestige. The reward for pleasing and for choosing to remain in Paradox and at Impasse is clear recognition of duty to act in a performance-rated state. Credence within Entity is desired or there could exist no Reason for culled imagination nor for continuing to use it as entertainment—like the performance of a paid puppet or craven hireling.

The subconscious has long been heralded as a thing of mystery and occult; a thing not easily understood; a supernatural retrieval pool for the fetishistic talismans of poets and artists.

The subconscious is the derivative of the incomplete and separated parallel of universal consciousness. It is the quagmire found on the last journey through the labyrinth of contrived mono-dimensional thought sequences. One must bring the Self forward of Intention for future tense. In order to live with the whole Self intact, one must exist in a Now state of sensual awareness applied to Reason, as messenger and interrogator. In this manner, Reason is not an active memory charge predetermined for the fixing of results as the product of resultant end manipulation. Such artifice, failsafed by suspect moral belief, is made to hold charge by word over sub-parallel, using the labyrinth of empowering words as cycling medium. This medium is usurper of Self. The fragile being that is human is shaped into a likeness that has little to do with his original humanity. Civilized man is his own creation, made in the image of his own supposition—machine-like, warring and estranged from his own genuinely nonaggressive nature that was obvious prior to word infestation.

Words, as implements for telling or as descriptive symbols to beget feeling, now exist as steadfast slick for the breeding of a future that uses the argot of sub-parallel for user identification with group, each failsafe shielded behind a disfigured and hypocritical seam that divides the Self from Self facade. The hypocrisy of life in the middle is the seeing without will to see; to feel and deny; to sense the color and bounty of life and to settle for Half Life and its drab and listless routine. Our hypocrisy is our Agreement to fail. Our hypocrisy is our willingness to hang in suspension between the sharp and ragged walls of The R.I.P. and our hypocrisy is our expectation of redemption.

The man who was called Christ sought to free humanity from the indignity of Self-negation and denial of life. According to Matthew 10:16-27, this is what Christ certainly realized as he watched man and woman make their transition into full use of the sub-parallel labyrinth of words. For as words were built into dutiful warrant, with prizes and rewards, the human race forfeited the wholeness of Self in favor of charged momentum and future promise. The masses of people were so adamant in their belief that Jesus Christ was their expected savior that they reasoned that all that could be required of them was to sit back and be saved.

However, salvation is not a thing that is easily gained. Redemption demands discipline that can be found only within the wholeness of Self. Once aware of Self, redemption, as promised by religion, is pointless.

As Christ used lexicon, he spoke to disarm Blame and to disentangle Blame Loop—to set people free as they claimed to free themselves from mediocrity and conformity. But people could not listen with feeling to the words of Christ. They followed him as though they hoped that their brains were sponges enough to absorb the necessary words to reveal what was, without feeling, quite beyond their grasp. Feeling is simple: It requires looking inward, and our hypocrisy will not tolerate that.

Transitioning feeling is passive growth. It is the absorption of word measure and responses and the removal of memory-implanted charged word motive to develop a whole sense that is emotional silence.

In Matthew, Christ speaks of variance. A man looks inward with feeling and knows the borderless joys of Self that are lasting and whole. The Self is beyond the boundaries of flesh, though not immortal. It ceases to exist when the body ceases to exist, for it belongs to flesh and blood. Heaven is a place of flesh and blood.

If able to enter a life of Self beyond the pale of Reason, there will be variance with family or job or community. In pas-

sive resolve, the Self has no allegiance to things except those
things which are specifically loyal to Self—beyond active memory concern.

Born into a life of Self, each human being is alone. In
Matthew, when Christ speaks of persecution, he speaks of persecution of those who reject the temporal rewards of a made-
meant-mean world of artifact for the chance to gaze inward at
the riches of Self.

Such persons cannot accept the paltry rewards set out for
them by Paradox. They cannot fall prey to the word labyrinth
because their feeling in Self precludes it. Self is its own reward,
and it creates and cultivates reward that is First Voice and cannot be subjugated and includes rewards of a spiritual and emotional nature as well as material rewards. No longer subject to
rule by Reason, such persons live life outside of The Agreement
Process. The price that they pay for so doing is their solitude
and their separateness.

Christ paid, with his life, the ultimate penalty for his ultimate
detachment. His crucifixion aptly illustrates that "by killing me,
you kill yourselves." The symbolic blood of Christ has lingered
for centuries.

The Self in feeling is able to hold affirmative respite from
Paradoxical Reason and is capable of suspending and dissolving
labyrinth with feeling to Reason in place that has no border.

Religion proclaims Heaven as the honored place for shareholders of awaited glory. Outside this Agreement in faith,
Heaven is Now or never. Place is the Self-essence in sensual
awareness.

Sensual awareness is total sense that includes all the senses
without the predominance of one or two that can appeal to verbal and written language.

The sense of touch crosses over words and is non-symbolic in
lexicon. Touch is received and known instantly because its
directness requires no translation. The beauty of touch is that it
involves all the senses.

In touch and taste and smell, there is no future. These three senses are excluded from the sub-parallel of words and are considered to be less important than sight and sound. But the tangible sense of touch is instantly recorded and reciprocally matched by sight. The sound of words is a distraction and part of the ailment that is assigned noun/verb–subject/predicate stance—that which presupposes another life that is held apart from the full matrix of sense.

This is life in the middle that has been erected for benefit of the arrogant word while the being essence is stillborn into still life and wasted. Waste is the resultant end of Paradox Reason.

This is Impasse by design for Reason manifest that yields knowledge for Blame. This is the paltry handed-down world of I-We-They in a made-meant-mean strata of word synthetic parallel—isolated from the human universal parallel of life consciousness within the total sense, housed inside an obsequious labyrinth of words for strategic advantage and power tactical devise for portions of Entity—that maintains its own systems logic: Paradox/Impasse for the parody of the undead.

The conundrum of the subconscious would not exist if the human being was whole, with full sensual capacity and a feeling, passionate essence. Reason would not exist as preface to Intent if the sub-parallel of words did not exist for synthetic provocation. As the developed word form indicates verb tense or pretense forward of the Now state, the conscious is turned inward to the subconscious until words become symbols in sub-parallel subconscious. The man-made mock real overlays two of the five senses, feeding mono-dimensional information, by sight and sound, to the being in partial fact altered state, producing a recorded artificial Truth that requires complete obedience and conformity for the further production of Truth.

We are mired in a cycle that is evidenced by the rerun tidal effect in which we relive taught portions of past circumstances that have been held in Reason for Reason in Impasse and promised promise. This is results for results. Thus, jobs for jobs becomes a matter of token payment for sacrifice falsely suffered and rerun for false suffering later. All the while, the diluted, cadaverous Self trembles in the aftermath of anxiety and obvious disorientation, forced into submissive mechanisms for hapless belief, icon worship for imagined cleansing and Self-fear subjected to political rule as the Self is torn to shreds by hero obligation and dependence.

Knowledge is a fear of fear strategy based on the Blame Loop. Fear is sold through education and law, stressing word dominance and earned authority with promise for proper symbolic upgrade for earning more. Higher education is the shelter given to the brotherhood of sapient shareholders in Reason. Colleges and universities are the caretakers of the means of Entity, nurseries for the undead in Half Life—the wholesale marketplace of results for results and jobs for jobs.

Business is reliant upon the sub-parallel of words almost exclusively as we approach the twenty-first century. Life in the middle is evolving into a slick fantastic in which the windows of Reason are smashed, with Reason becoming an uncontrolled and unreliable vehicle steered by correct think-factory muscle. The safeguard of law controls only the illusion of fear. The human being cannot transition fear once legal imposition is set and must continually relive fear through word containment and legal enthrallment.

The right to fairness is, then, the right to suppression of an alleged wrong, when a crime is Self-determinate always. Law does not forbid anger and hatred, for these things are built into The Agreement Process for use. Law does punish, but not as much as it sanctions. Agreement conditions its adherents to react for cause. Provocation is implanted and response is encouraged and condoned. Reason, as justice, is blind, and Intention, as arbiter, is obtuse.

Life in the middle is the massive embodiment of word implant and think-process. Words are the symbolic subconscious impetus that act as Reason. To say that the word "subconscious" designates the mind beneath or beyond the conscious one is to use word imposition to enact or underscore The R.I.P. Totality of the universal parallel is not the subconscious at all but the sum total of consciousness that The R.I.P. disengages and prohibits. The tear in the total sensual consciousness of the human being is the sub-parallel of words split like empty husks from the fullness of feeling and passion, used as detriment to the bright center of Self to make of it a slave and a barterer for the figments of momentum and time.

There is no subconscious realm. There is only Now.

Progress is the emblematic exchange of Reason/Intention, as provoked by word imposition in a made-meant-mean altered state of past, present and future tense.

Progress is a misnomer, for the inner being that is the Self resides in Now. In Now, there are no prizes. In Now, Self is the prize.

Enjoining the process of word prehension is the giving of allegiance to a pre-designed and implemented state of mind which assumes power of the arrogant over the meek. Survival of the fittest is by word use only, for we all know that the only thing truly worthy of survival is the microscopic virus that will survive all that we attempt to destroy it.

Our fitness and mastery, as a specie, is conjecture and supposition drawn from tactical supremacy, technological stuffing and scientifically paid-for analysis.

Paradox cannot work, nor can it justify anything more than positions installed, taken and validated in Reason. Paradox feeds upon itself and humanity is left to run on empty. This is blind end and perfect snare. This is Paradox created by knowledge at Impasse.

Subconscious is word manifest. Thinking is performed with words and exists for Intention only: a hypotaxis. *Realization*—by introspection—and *precognition* are words that describe total sensual bathing: Sixth Sense composite use expressed emotionally. Paradox belongs to the conscious/subconscious parallel of written/verbal input: Without memory enhancement, Paradox cannot exist. Impasse is the limited use of two senses for reciprocation of cause and effect for Intention and for further word impetus. Knowledge is the assignment of the sub-parallel, by words, to presuppose action intended for predestined fixing of a mental state applied: last Reason held for last Reason used. The Sixth Sense is the ultimate interrogation system for mind/body unity: Reason is digested. Sixth Sense is a composite of feeling below The R.I.P.: A hypostatic union. Sixth Sense recognizes the futility of Impasse/Paradox by its stricture and confinement to a predestined cause-and-effect way of life. Peace of mind is the full matrix of the senses united. Subconscious is the realm of the implanted sub-parallel and does not exist except in sub-parallel. To feel to Reason is the transit to open to the Now state. The Now state is non-doubt and leaves the mask of Intention behind as it leaves words behind—as empty shells: the symbols we fill to achieve designated roles in noun/verb advantage.

Life in the middle is life inside the parameters of Paradox that is Intentionally held at Impasse; that is made by Agreement only. Progress is the false sense of time created by word application that has only one flat-line dimension.

We are unable to reconcile symbols with our senses, for the senses perceive things directly. In the split of The R.I.P., our manner of perception is limited to two senses only, and we make mean that blue matches sky and green matches tree when these things are symbolic only—relayed by sight and sound—and are not tactile. We abide in a word that is either/or—of deference or Blame.

The senses are innately whole and complete without the use of words and they remain mute, and as such, belong only to the realm of emotion, the language of the senses—stripped down to the language of the heart. Man is the most gentle and caring creature on earth, vaulted inside a Paradox by everyone's Agreement to do so.

NOTES

NAME: DATE:

X

X

THOUGHT

Doubt: Zero Space and Natural Space

The reasonable man adapts himself to the world;
the unreasonable one persists in trying to adapt the world
to himself. Therefore all progress depends on
the unreasonable man.

—George Bernard Shaw

THOUGHT IS NOT CONFORMATION. It is the unending collection of continuing sensual inquiry into the human mind, which is not always willing to be probed and explored. Thinking is a matter of seriously reflected consciousness and of a consciousness that, when brought to task for its causes and effects, recoils upon itself and pushes back to all that it knows—to all that is inductive and breaching. From this break—this chasm in consciousness—is born Intention. Nothing is misconstrued, but forced across an altered state distance measured in spans of desire for Reason to be completed.

It is easy to confuse having been taught with learning and to confuse time with Future. All are illusions of Reason and are disposable. It is interesting to run a gauntlet in trespass of areas that have long been Knowledge failsafed and closed, strung with emotional signal flares—neural and cerebral traps.

Revolution is not necessary. There is no need to set off searing blazes in renunciation and insurrection nor in admonishment of Reason for Reason, for this is method of war and makes fact of manufactured Truth for belief. Truth for Reason makes of the human being a preternatural predator in lustful pursuit of any promised miracle and metaphysically hungry for the kill. Blame shears him of his inherent humility and hones him as a weapon most select and valued for Reason made that is pernicious and baneful. Militia are banded and cohered for Reason. Disregard is excuse. The time machine called human has become a governed and lawful demigod of future past, bought and sold as corporeal pestilence, his fleshiness undone, his arrogance, at last, humbled. Half Life legislated is a plague of tyranny that consumes. By dictate of law, the human being is born dead and bound over for process.

Thinking is process and does not become thought until Reason is doubted and dissolved into feeling. This is Reason to Reason and feeling to resolve through sensual Self-interrogation that stems from the naturally fluid and organically unlawful silence that is human emotion.

Thought is neither an act nor an art. Through doubt, Reason is transited to reciprocal feeling until, by deduction of Reason, feeling is Resolved. The transition of Reason to feeling is signaled by sensations of discomfort and unease. We have been trained to desire Reason, and when our desires are manifested as Reason, we succumb to the anxiety that ensues by longing for Reason or by loving for Reason or hating for Reason or negating for Reason. If one is fairly aware of Self, such anxiety may be heard or felt as a bumping or crashing sensation—a tumbling that summons tears or integumental flushing or paleness; a tightening of muscles—as Reason and feeling collide. If one succumbs to Reason, one acts in favor of Reason, the social virtue.

Virtue is the given right to invalidate Self-cognizance, and this renunciation is justified, its consequences softened by the sanctioned morals of marriage and allegiance and belief. Denial of Self is rewarded with future promise.

How easily the human being is yoked and how cheaply is he ransomed and traded! Virtue is a parsimonious ruler and its subjects are vanquished to dwell in the heavily seeded air of time. The virtuous bondsman is incarcerated by remorse and pursuit and hope, sentries at the bounds of an attenuated altered state that is governed and enforced by tense. The moral chattel, disposed to Impasse/Reason process-think, makes valuations and culmination based upon patrimonial false suffering and a legacy of repentance.

How low to the ground we must crawl to taste of the muck that oozes down to us from centuries of contrition! The weight of tradition alone subdues us. Is it no wonder that in religion, the symbolic personification of ultimate evil and heinous transgression is the serpent who creeps along the earthly floor bemired and sullied and begrudged? From whom do we recoil and for what do we repent? Is not repentance the laying low of the human essence; the choking off of an empyreal voice; the shattering of exquisite compound vision into sharp, jagged fragments of terror that rend and puncture?

Repentance is the ripping of majestic will. We kill the human beast and, through Self-hatred and posited faith in a heritage of fable, embrace deception as the measure of divine Truth. Symbolically, we become what is predicated by false subscription to slanted value as we slide and worm our way along the face of the earth, ever the dastardly victim and cunning servant of virtue.

As fair implements of virtuous deception, we sell misery to the miserable while making a living from the proceeds, and we name this progress and social good and future. Whom do we serve? When does service become empowerment and when does empowerment become larceny? What is license but license to inveigle and cheat? The human being is plumbed and reamed by psychology, politics, education, law and religion; followed blindly by medicine, commerce, industry, research and technology.

What is group hate? What is ideational tomfoolery in the name of Agreement? We tear down: We revere future and emulate past, with never so much as a glance at what is always lost in Now. If time is always a measure of what is past and future, what can future bring? Atonement for the past? If so, time is halted and Reason has no carrier. The human being, encapsulated in time, looks "through a glass darkly"; accepts partial fact; and lives in the dull traces of Half Life—never within the fullness of his being, never "face to face."

The human condition is a functioning Paradox that requires institutional thought imposition: Impasse, the last place in deadlock; terminal cincture; Blame Loop redux; determinative results for results. Impasse is the vermiculate and gnarled appendix to Reasoned process-think and the blind end at the passage to absolute space—place without object.

Acceptable reality has but a single dimension that is matte and flat. Intelligence makes use of sameness. Intelligence is the pervasive hole that demands a connection between subjective matter and matter itself. As Provoker Function, Intelligence educes matter to mono-dimension when matter exists in absolute space quite without either subject or predicate. The human being, in altered state, shrinks the world around him as he shrinks himself. Through a hazy, mirrored image of contorted Self, he obscures and disparages nature with formula.

Thought that is not critical is the mental binding and tying up of a spare and fragile creature. It is method for containment. It is a lessening of original will and a diluent of the senses. The human being suffers falsely behind a thin disguise, and in his suffering is a stranger to himself, an alien confined to a world of alien things. Thought is imposition.

In elementary symbolic thought, there are no definitive completions; no concise and whole points of view. There are partial summations and partial descriptions. Completeness of thought is an emotional state and is encoded in so much sensual dimension that flat-line focus and function become impossible. Thus, reason is, *a priori*, a presumption and pre-emption before whole fact and before whole or original will. Reason separates mind and body and mind relies upon Intention for enactment of archetypal, handed-down, pre-meant wants and needs that have been designated acceptable by civilized altered state. Half Life is mandatory.

What may be intelligence in the human being is innate and passive. Innate intelligence slowly infuses information to deduce and clarify Self in resolve. We should never confuse innate intelligence with intellectual allegiance to pre-conditions and obedience to regulations and law. Such allegiance and obedience are counter-reactions made from fear of fear and are enforced when one accepts living conditions that are cycled for advantageous ordering and possession. With such acceptable intelligence is obedience used in deliberate ignorance to perpetuate Agreeable ignorance.

As current Reason decays, new knowledge is invented and housed in instructive blocks from which the latest formulas are commercially meted out and sold. Intellect, as measure of achievement and merit, always current, is a commodity. Intellect is remembrance of the method of progress handed down and dependent upon results and time as meters of consumption and breakdown. All measures lead to the blind end of fear of fear; Impasse; last Reason held; the appendix to thought. Impasse is the crux of The R.I.P. that tears Reason from feeling and breaches the universal parallel: Impassionment

Shorn of feeling and pressed forward, thought is afterthought, and what could be life is confined to after-time and left to dangle in emptiness untouched, unseen, unheard. Is it, somehow, far easier to mourn the death of the human animal than to ever venture beyond fear into the depths of a sea of life? Far easier to pay a price than to step out of The Agreement Process of tomorrow *ad infinitum*? Easier to die a thousand deaths without ever once having lived? To never open to the warmth and splendor of a picturesque and consonant world? To always barter and trade for Half Life and Still Life and promise of life when life, with all explicit bounty and joy, is at hand Now with no premium due and no redemption necessary?

Within the hard standards of mechanical time, we have reached a critical juncture in the use and misuse of Reason manifest. Before we came to this place of dull pain and hate,

humankind used Reason, but as an isolated implement for symbolic understanding, while still realizing that something very
specific and reliable underlay all Reasons made. But in the age
of technological Titanism, Reason is undifferentiated. We walk
rapidly in one door and out another without once stopping to
realize that what is made to mean is not meant to mean anything. Reason was a means of inspecting and lightly ordering a
temporal and tempestuous world and not an end unto itself
that, with its onerous protocol has become overbearing in its
regulatory demands for uniformity of pre-conditioned afterthought and that has a vast autocratic reach.

The human being, with innate intelligence, has always been
able to see the eyes behind the eyes of human feeling that is
the genesis of life. Inside feeling, there is multidimensional
intelligence that knows no punishment; is not exacting nor critical nor jealous; carries no malice—no hateful and secretive
weight of either money or trade. The multidimensional intelligence of the human being is silent; it moves along silent paths
to soft cerebral fields and, in the pliancy of the mental soil, sets
strong roots that probe and imbibe. Innate multidimensional
intelligence knows no bounds and fears no fear; is spherical
and turns slowly on its sensorial axis; changes; adjusts; knows
well its emotional seasons; and knows well its sentient tilt, always
tacitly resolute and of present regard.

From the moment that we are born, we feel. Reason is
nowhere in sight. Hunger, thirst and physical comfort are basic
needs. There is no pretense nor falseness in the human infant's
cry to be held and nurtured through flesh and blood kinship
with other human beings. No elaborate scheme of language is
necessary. An infant responds to touch and smell automatically
and it knows that the smell of its mother means nourishment
and that her touch, therefore, brings comfort. The emotional
bonding of mother and child is accomplished through the
senses. Reason cannot establish this. Reason says, "She is my
child, therefore I must love her." But love that is to last a life-

time has no Reason. The senses say, "You are the child of my body or not. This does not matter. What matters is my touch of you, my looking at you, my listening to your cry. I nourish you with my feeling, which is born of the blending of our senses beyond all Reason."

Past the stage of infancy, we learn to feign love for Reason. There may be special treatment or certain prizes or active involvement with another human being's objectives, which we take as our own. What we cheat ourselves into believing to be love is the relinquishing of Self for Reason. There is, in love for Reason, no eyes-behind-the-eyes fullness of feeling that admits no jealousy, no loss, no malice, no dread, no confinement, no quick overturn of love into hate or love into habituation.

In love wrought for Reason, there is the reasonable demand for what is right and good. Love for right Reason becomes a brandishing of status, with flattering tags and earned badges of Reasonable love failsafed by right through the craft and the power of state. Indeed, love that is deemed right and good is certified and licensed by state and sanctioned by the church— the very vehicles of Entity that claim to vouchsafe our redemption through a God that has long ago been sucked dry of the waters of life—and to vouchsafe our Agreement through promise when the promise of Agreement has long ago proven to be the promise of Agreed nightmare, bound in lowness of repentance for a prostrate tomorrow.

What manner of thought enters the ganglia of the serpentine belly that is the countenance of the human brain in Agreement? Is it thought or active memory of thought? We are governed by automatic responses that elude us and by incorporated and axiomatic blocks of sold fear that we grind and mill and cycle for use and reuse. We hold ourselves aloof from nature by virtue of divine will to sapience. How can we claim variance from cyprinids who swim through sluggish and cloudy waters to snatch at wet crumbs? How superior are dwellers within the acrid and styptic cisterns of progress/time to blindfish who, by natural selection, live in the black waters of caves, their eyes without function and their sense of sight regressed?

What hallmarks the locus of human devolution? With every technological advance, we forfeit to mechanization the rounded dimensions of an intelligent Self and the pristine beauty of a finite world. The noise and sloth of a haranguing and dogmatic language beleaguer our senses. The word is made surrogate for emotion, and its platitudes and clichés are made Truth, and Truth does not matter as long as there is Agreement to made fact. Like a blindfish in a cave, Retrograde Man relinquishes his sensorial awareness for Reason.

Retrograde Man assuages and denies the loss of his senses through invention. We take pride in our ability to mentally swoop and swirl like flying dervishes in a cybernetic swoon on the thin margins of electronic air. Retrograde Man, in dearth of a material God, finds the electric brain, in its immensity, an apt substitute. It feeds and anoints us, and its charged impulses rule and impose. The electric brain, woven from fibrous tubes of light and bent in direction upon direction like a geodesic dome, encircles a race of mortal hybrids inside a field of exposed and slender impulses. The human race has replaced itself with mere flurries of beeps and flutters. Survival of a species is determined by random numbers on a punchboard of colored points and non-human utterances; by stiff hands on a chimerical clock; by feeling to Reason circumvented; by coded scraps from the refuse of a cloven mind.

The mind of an animal is sensual and complete with working stimulation intact. The mind of an animal has no use for Reason. The human being's marked asset is his ability to Reason with feeling. Is it not perversely inhuman that we deliberately choose to channel ourselves away from original Self to favor the mind in R.I.P.?

The will to ignorance is our one volitive act, and we act in pretense to a bewildering sagacity.

NOTES

NAME: DATE:

XI

XI

CRITICAL THINKING

Discernment, Integrity, Resolve

The state is a state of Slavery in which a man
does what he likes to do in his spare time
and in his working time that which is required of him.

—Eric Gill

INTELLIGENCE IS TRIUMPH OVER MATTER. Intelligence shapes
and delegates matter to purpose and reasons purpose into
oblique gratification of cardinal need. Gaunt cords of bound
cerebral indigence and poverty prevail over substance until a
contradictory premium of satisfaction or dissatisfaction is
attained: Positive blackout or vainglorious constraint.

When we question momentum of intellectual construct and
its acquisitions from mastery of substance, we find that complacency has concluded critical thinking.

Critical thinking is capital deliberation and regard—through
verdict and decision—that outline the acicular parameters of
Self. Without such trenchant and acuminate definition of Self,
the essence of the human creature is in peril. In the interest of
vigilance, it must be said that all thinking is critical unless it is
not thought at all but is think-process. Think-process is both a
symptom and a mechanism of extinction: the pending annihilation of the human mind.

Critical thinking is ceno-sight into extemporaneous capacity—
the unfolding of the Self into burnished and glistening Feeling to
Reason through radically attentive cues; the signals and imprints
of doubt; and the Reason to Reason of ceno-think. Made thought

is removed from critical thought when it is matched and removed from a parallel of intended design and embedded within a prodigal parallel that is the passive human mind.

Ultimate thought is resolute doubt that can be realized down to the reciprocal of zero space. So deeply rooted are beliefs in codes of right and wrong—of truth and of virtue—that the human being has rendered himself nearly incapable of critical thought. We are the ignorant and artful spouters of doctrine and comparison: the wielders of the double-edged sword of Reason. We are secure believers in justice. Justified thought dictates rectitude as dire need and Retrograde Man solicits equity and buys it through custom of strategy. Stripped of such banality in restraint, the human organism must bear question. Interrogation is unauthorized and think-factory exempt. Outside Agreement, there is no Reason for justified thought. Critical thought does not require justification. The critical thinker stands alone and his intelligence is consummate.

Credence is repentance: The human being, in R.I.P., expects absolution through Belief. The human being, in R.I.P., trusts. Trust is failsafe and sanction; partial deception, by manifest word. It is Impasse Reason through blind end and suffocation of the human essence. Trust is the hallmark of our Agreement to fail and the failure of the human being is his will to trust and his will to Believe.

To allow oneself to become an object of Belief is to procure eternal death. The hoax of immortality is brutal and destructive. Christ was destined for crucifixion because Belief dictated it by merit. Christ, as a living being, defied belief. Murdered, the symbol of Christ became the sanction of Belief and was sanctioned into Belief. Religion worships and exalts Belief; smugly exults in its own postulated and invented credulity.

Belief is the specious and false redeemer of mankind: There is no messiah more mighty than iron-clad dogma. Belief in Christ is Belief in Antichrist.

Deduced by doubt and without justification of deed or think

process, religion is exposed down to its rigid and hardened pith; as it directs its allegiants to act as pilferers and looters of human substance; in the names of right and good and God. The strangling of the human essence, in religious R.I.P., is God-conditioned and God-approved: Annihilation saves. Thought is Reciprocity in Paradox. Thought is apostasy.

We must ask: How can The Creature called human profess profound belief in a God of love and in the myth of a loving savior when he, with vehemence and expedience, exercises his own accrued and bought tenets as will to destruction? Is this Paradox?

How mired are we in ignoble lowness of repentance through credulity that we R.I.P. the fiber of that which could be like God? Is calamity the same as justice? In use of Paradoxical lexicon, an inverted noun serves no purpose other than antithesis to feeling. A word is like a thing perched upon an edge to a deep cerebral shaft that, once uttered, flutters down into the enigma that is the manifold looking glass of the human mind. As the mind attempts to decipher symbolic density, structure is mutated until the word, as discarnate token, is inverted, its encoded subterranean significance quite opposed to its made-meant-mean altered state definition in Provoker Function. Memory, then, carries its circumstance to completion. Blame is virtue in memory.

The essential basic nature of the mind is to question: Variance and vicissitude and shifting frictions are the vehicles of creation and transition. Question is the seeker of symmetry and the finder of parallel and match, beyond Reason. The mind is a riddler, and it finds pleasure in its inverted analogues by opposition. Disagreement is homage.

Outside lexicon, and through a reflection that is the mind, words are stripped of made meaning. Made symbols assume myriad shapes when filtered through the channels of passive memory. Justifications are noted and clarifiers are distinguished. Those who justify think-process ignore noun inversions and aver dogma of partial truth. This is the split of Self and the split of life into Half Life.

Critical probing through introspection finds reciprocal mental matches in life below The R.I.P. until sensual feeling, through parallel match, can be defined as thought.

Dearth of critical thought subjects the human being to the prosaic grayness of Half Life within The Agreement Process in which nouns are Agreed to mean. Husbands and wives and justice and ascetics are all accepted and touted, by lexicon, as valid things, while the inversions of such nouns are overtly decried. Agreed meaning castigates all that the passive mind finds no Reason to rebuke.

Beneath The R.I.P., the mind recognizes no wife and no whore, no husband nor pander, no calamity, no justice. A wife is harlot and harlot is wife as long as there is the Agreed thin veil of belief and as long as there is capricious hoax.

Beneath the R.I.P., there are no masks. Animadversion function sanctions no guise. Active memory—trained artifice—may be tricked by belief, but one cannot trick the minotaur, beast and man, who has lived too long in the pit of the labyrinth, ill-fed on the sacrifices of life for Half Life—of Life for word.

Beneath The R.I.P.; beneath cerebral cabal and plot; beneath the reflecting chambers of the mind that, by inversion of icon, can unmask and reveal full meaning of analogue through opposition; beneath the fissured decoder of truth; beneath convoluted riddle; and beneath cortical beast; we may approach parametric vacuity, or the place that is not a place: Intrinsic void, life center, open, unfixed and bathed in sensual accord.

There is no intellectual measurement for void that is infinite. Infinity has no basis in Reasonable concept: Space is sensually dazzling and clear. Feeling, in place void of Reason, is parametric only by the limits of a single, exhaustible life. Beyond one organism lie millions, constantly in flux of beginning and end until sensual reach becomes boundless.

Language behind language, or noun density inversion, is

Sixth Sense: speaking through the emotional Self. When we refuse to recognize the cryptic symbology of our own dynamic minds, we placate active memory, which makes of us the puppetry of Entity and use. Volition is made exclusive to monolithic We construct and is restricted to the I of We for enactment.

The human being has no will. Law becomes us—the rank and file who have no resolve except that empowered by investiture or entrusted, franchised vote. We are the sad, gray proletariat from vanquished race and conquered tribe.

The subconscious dilemma is an altered state mental construct from Impasse that is a renunciation of intrinsic void and passive parallel thought. Subconscious denotes a place of dreams as divided from a place of living, when all symbology is analogous and harmonic through critical thought. Human consciousness is not divided except as we believe.

We believe in allegiance to The R.I.P. We consume and are consumed. We nullify and are nullified.

Forward of Self pursuits are out of alignment to feeling/Reason resolve. Intention is the dissimulating snare of resultant end Reason for Reason. To Reason, by analogous opposition and match, is to enter critical thought, where there can be no justification for acts opposed to Self-parallel—a contempt of Self for Reasons added and emotion subtracted.

Blame Loop is rightful adhesion. If we do not believe in right, then, we are believers in wrong, and wrong becomes right. Morality, as mental bound, is machination and group process-think. Process-think is subject to caprice and changes its tenets constantly for Reason. Blame is formed in a circle to enable its believers to always find Reason for blame, like riders on a carousel who reach to pull a ring. Word is the power of Entity.

Blame is vanguard of justice, and justice is expediter for right and claim, end unto end, until substance is consumed. Life is a business; misery for profit; dignity for sale.

But is business life? We have made business life to insure safety from life when there is no life. We are consumed by a knowledge-based system enacted to preserve rights. Below The R.I.P., there is no Reasonable freedom to be purchased for equity of a virtuous bondsman. We are trapped as long as we uphold divine promise of parole. We cannot break our chains as long as we Agree to suffer. Fear of fear is Agreed salvation through Agreed temperance. Citizens in Half Life above The R.I.P. palliate with the promise of freedom from fear and live in Impasse apotheosis: the idolatrous failsafe of asylum mock-God, ruler of the word and ruler of Entity momentum.

Freedom is resolution of fear.

Retrograde Man, the moral slave in the circular chronicle of future past, clings to the thralldom of Reasonable fear. Master who lives in fear of fear, for share in its manifest of fear of thought, is slave. In non-life that is Half Life, virtue is blame. This is the severity of our holy-mock no-consequence belief system and our licit method of trial by warrant: *We* manifest is suicide by homily. All groups are dangerous.

Critical thought is the conscious door to freedom. Freedom is capacity to renounce the parameters of Half Life. To fall through the smooth reflective walls of the mind is a fall through Reason and a shattering of fable: an awakening to sad intelligence. Beyond the breaking probe is the puzzle of reciprocal match; life without despair; the mending of The R.I.P.; and the transport of the human being to Impassionment—sensorial inferno.

Critical thought is the mental valve that, when turned, clarifies and educes devout attention to Self. To live life fully is to attend to the immeasurable spheres of Self.

In R.I.P., no system of Reason can exist without the Entity of Agreement and no state of feeling is certified to exist except by terminal belief in synthetic circumstance, which is Agreement for Reason. Sapient specie is vised and clamped in Impasse, where meaning control is finite meaning manufactured slick and made to mean. There is no meaning: Definition renders meaning unnecessary.

Thought, in a world of process think, is maverick and opposed. There is no nexus between thought and non-thought; no mitigation and no relief. In the reflecting chambers of the existential mind, death is not the antithesis of life in Paradox. Death is thought inversed for Reason.

In lexicon, all words are The Word and The Word is doctrine. God came from The Word and Entity is God-word in conscripted Blame. The Word is usurper of feeling and the thief who robs himself. Reason for Reason is flawed, its fissures grown wide and commodious. Reason lexicon is protuberant and excrescent. Reason is both mastermind and consumption of Retrograde Man, mock-anthropoid with protonic pinions. He is a thing made up.

Feeling is manipulated and made to mean, made to believe— made credulity Reasoned for made misery. There is no truth beyond Self-feeling unreasoned.

There is a place, in balanced middle, where Reason and feeling are symbiotic; where feeling is not charged with belief nor system and Reason is elective and without blame. There is no consciousness beyond the senses; no subconscious and no divisions of ego, superego and id. Fear of fear is fear of Self. Fear of fear is the split and the breach in the human parallel of consciousness.

Fear is Reason inverted. When fear becomes friend, there is no Reason for blame. When fear becomes friend, Reason and feeling are resolved.

Blame Loop is Paradox, and Impasse is think-factory for justification of blame. Will the human being surpass all circles and straight lines? Humankind is not guilty of anything other than ignorance and Self-bondage: Through his ignorance and bondage, he is not worthy of guilt. Shame is in future, in Retrograde devolution: the mental undoing, orgiastic cunning and facile hoax.

Man and woman are unnatural enemies, their latent sexuality purloined by deed and trust into subjugation.

Sex is for Reason and worth a fortune in suffering and conflict.

Through critical thought and probe, the human being trusts nothing but Self, and this he interrogates to discretionary fear. Fear is friend: We have no enemy except We who devise.

Paradoxical Reason is slipping into overload and strain. Nonsense is sense, and The Word is paramount to the point that it does not matter that any personal choice is accomplished nor that any product is sold. Only matters that which is concluded by The Word: Intention.

Correction malfunction, due to overworked tolerances, is a huge side business in drugs and therapies. Psychology prospers as factory logic disintegrates. Mental sickness is invented to fit scientific credo. However, critical thought, as Self-probe, reveals the human being as tenacious and steadfast—a creature as authentic as his heartbeat is resolute and adamant.

Homo Sapiens is the most gentle creature on earth, but is made angry by a system of knowledge that is impoverished and reduced to standardized parody by word slick. In future that we cannot afford, "To be or not to be," will not be a choice. In future, "To be" will be the domain of the contemptible delusive and the acceptable insane. Reason will invert upon itself until Reason is preposterous.

Progress is a prize that can no longer be won. Each step forward is ten steps backward for Retrograde Man in the world of latter day R.I.P.

When will the human being learn to dream the perfect dream: the one dream that continues its perfection even after the eyes are open? Can we dream a dream of perfection that is beyond hope and beyond Belief, beyond trust and obeisance, beyond justice? Can we dream the dream of Self that requires no law and seeks no remedy? Can we dream the dream of Self that has no bounds? We imagine all manner of contortion and misery. How can it be more hurtful to imagine all that can be but is not Now?

How painful is the probe to Self?

NOTES

NAME: DATE:

There exists the contention, both biblical and inherent to Reason,
that there is a path or road that is, explicitly, the path of the Senses
or Feeling. On this path, neither Conscience nor Reason matter.
Both are abstracts that resemble Potential To Feeling as Feeling is
given Voice. Visually, we recognize this:

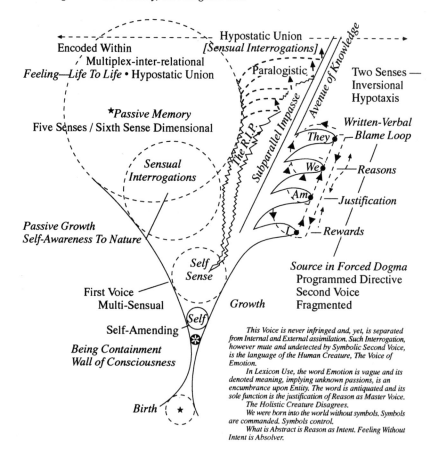

Hypostatic Union
[*Sensual Interrogations*]

Encoded Within
Multiplex-inter-relational
Feeling—Life To Life • Hypostatic Union

Paralogistic

Two Senses —
Inversional
Hypotaxis

★*Passive Memory*
Five Senses / Sixth Sense Dimensional

Avenue of Knowledge

The R.I.P.

Subparallel Impasse

Written-Verbal
They —*Blame Loop*

Sensual
Interrogations

We —*Reasons*

Am —*Justification*

Passive Growth
Self-Awareness To Nature

I —*Rewards*

Self
Sense

Source in Forced Dogma
Programmed Directive
Second Voice
Fragmented

First Voice
Multi-Sensual

Growth

Self

Self-Amending

Being Containment
Wall of Consciousness

This Voice is never infringed and, yet, is separated
from Internal and External assimilation. Such Interrogation,
however mute and undetected by Symbolic Second Voice,
is the language of the Human Creature, The Voice of
Emotion.
  In Lexicon Use, the word Emotion is vague and its
denoted meaning, implying unknown passions, is an
encumbrance upon Entity. The word is antiquated and its
sole function is the justification of Reason as Master Voice.
  The Holistic Creature Disagrees.
  We were born into the world without symbols. Symbols
are commanded. Symbols control.
  What is Abstract is Reason as Intent. Feeling Without
Intent is Absolver.

Birth

XII

───── XII ─────

INTELLIGENCE, THE CREATURE

Multidimensional Interrogative Before Fear Is Built

The word is the Verb, and the Verb is God.

—Victor Hugo
Contemplations

Rᴇᴛʀᴏɢʀᴀᴅᴇ Mᴀɴ ғᴏʀᴍᴜʟᴀᴛᴇs ғɪxᴇᴅ ᴄᴏɴᴄʟᴜsɪᴏɴ from oath and axiom as determining limits of Reason for Reason perplexity that comprises Half Life invariant in positive R.I.P. The will to penalty is heritage miscarried. To look toward future past with a rigid eye is to see, without yielding, the contingency of restraint when there can be no restraint but restraint made and made again. The jealous slave does not envy unimpeded dignity as a thing to be coveted but as a thing to be destroyed. Fear is not friend to the bondsman. Fear is friend to the beast. Wrought honor is the domain of the savage. Bestowed honor is the emblem of the weak.

Retrograde peers through caviling eyes at the world of the animal, compares himself, and deems himself conqueror by surmise and exaction of purpose. Within the sanguinary censures of bondage, animal life is valueless unless value is defined by atrocity. The human Creature, in guise of resplendent serpent in repentant malediction, is both master and slave to himself. Retrograde reviled is the pride of man and hope is his decoy. False value is the virtue of suffering: All suffering is false. The righteous value of good is atrocity and the perfection of shame is ideal. Upon the reflected split that is the intelligence of The

Creature in R.I.P., pride and shame are reciprocal, and there is
no balance. All hope and promise are intentional malice and
are institutional. Upon word slick, the Self of man slides away.
Pride of the bondsman is built upon foundations of shame.

Animals that are deemed lower than man cannot impose
upon themselves the value of good. They have not the capacity
for good nor the capacity for knowledge. The world of The
Creature is sensorial, and its perceptions are uncluttered and
unimpeded by made thought and the split of Impasse. The
Creature lives below The R.I.P.—in the hinterlands of the mind
that once were the occult realms of man, unbridled and
untamed.

Retrograde lives upon the picked carrion of civilization. He
becomes soft. He robs The Creature of its teeth. What is Intelligence without substance? What is certificate except devaluation
that is assigned value? Who pays the price for the mental undoing of The Creature called human? What dour bargain drives
the Self-annihilator?

The sentient man does not require purposeful explanation.
He is ever merciful of mystery and doggedly questioning of
faith. Faith contains no mystery because its tenets are taught
and presumed. The idolater is caught in a sound web of faith
that restrains him from the very mystery for which he proclaims
faith. He claims that faith is his lamp unto the world. But what
is light to a blind man? The sentient has no fear of darkness,
for fear is his friend and bears luminosity for no one. The sentient is eyeless by choice and savors worn blackness before the
promise of sight. Sight and sound are the bearers of mirage and
the dictum of faith. In the darkness of fear, there is no shrill of
a redeeming trumpet, and no lighted path. Retrograde, in
R.I.P., lives in a sensorial world of one dimension or two. He is
in favored Agreement with The Voice of It. Two senses serve
him well, for he sees to abominate and hears to blame. Retrograde, the bondsman, cannot taste and touch and smell except
as warranted by Agreement in sight and sound. For Retrograde,

there is no picture untainted by Reason and no intonation that is not ingrained in Paradox. Green tree is as imbedded and imprinted on the human brain as is the will to Paradoxical dubiety: How can there be faith when there has been no doubt?

In Paradox, faith and doubt are reciprocals. Human Intelligence, the stillborn, is disallowed. The Creature is dead at birth. When viewed through the insuperable recoiling lenses of the mind at Impasse, the number of reciprocals can never balance to zero. In Paradox there is no void, for alternate values fall in unending succession like dominoes. Faith is belief in dogma, while doubt is belief in nothing.

Yet doubt is exacting. In doubt, one must pay the penalty of sadness, while happiness costs nothing. Doubt is exacting enough that it becomes faith exhumed.

Faith asks nothing of the human being except group determination: virtual slavery. There is safety in numbers. What is true in black is also true in white: What we believe, we can as easily disbelieve, and values do not last. In reciprocation of value, we devalue the nothing of Self that is the complete resolution of human will. The Voice of It precludes the will of the cipher. Faith is Self murder. Doubt is zero destiny.

The will to zero is recognition of value reciprocals as bearers of the same Intent. Entering zero space, sentient man detects the clear image of hate unto love that is an exact replica of love except that it spawns desire. Desire is caprice. To love for Reason is hate reciprocated. Love beyond Reason is not subjective. Love that is beyond Reason, with no value reciprocal, has no bounds: It is pure human emotion. Beyond value, the human being is incapable of hate.

What is pledge but Reason? The eyes and the ears can be deceiving. The bondsman is ensnared by dutiful sight and sound. The beginnings of life are vast and regionless. We cheat ourselves with echo and mirage and we cheat ourselves with duty to The Word. What is Provoker Function? Who is The Great Deceiver? Of what do we repent?

We repent our humanity.

To crawl outside the edges of law and into the open sectors of lawlessness is to become wholly human. The lawless do not maim and kill and rob. It is the lawful who plunder. A common thief adheres strictly to the dictates of rule, and all trespassers are followers.

Who and what designates barriers? In Half Life, with full use of law and control, all pillage is predictable. This is lawful intent. Like rats in a maze, we are channeled into obedience and trained to submit. We are taught that secure chains of enactment are placed for valid Reason, and we believe without doubt in our bondage. We define our lives by the security of our chains and we pay a price.

Outside the palisade of law, sentient man is Self-adjusting. He keeps no written record of blame as Reason nor of law as penalty. Justice is Reason to profit from blame.

Intelligence, The Creature, is the untamed Self. Innate human intelligence is a gift from creator to created. Intelligence is the mythic infidel incarnate. In an embodied state of doubt, how can we fear?

Fear is the unreciprocated benediction of doubt. To what do we present icons and symbols? All symbology is token favor in retribution of fear. We fear life and mask it in symbolic placation. We perform, for Reason, to seek reprisal and requital from fear. Prayer is an act of supplication in hope of reprisal from fear: Hope is vain.

There is no hope. Fear is Now, and fear is finite. Why seek the infinite of Why when there are no answers? Solution is pacification and the infinite of Why is a facade. Reason triumphs as intelligence, The Creature, recoils: The beast will not attend its own suicide.

Before zero magnitude is entrance to a giant tangle in which is contained the solid trail of where and when and how and what of the Why infinite. Reason and intellect and the core of knowledge are pulled into this webbed space; are shrunken and demure shapes in the rhythmic wake of that which is peaceful and calm and clear before filling. Providence is a fair sea of untroubled waters. Providence is the last reducible serenity. There is no equation for God.

Providence is both creator and vessel of creation. Faith is but a yardstick to measure that which cannot be measured and a means to an inverted end.

Doubt is immeasurable. Doubt, by its enormity, reduces knowledge and reason to zero match and opens The Creature to the fountainhead of natural sense and the threads that bind to creation and to the parallel of life.

In parallel match, the reflected imprints of Sixth Sense corollary and inversion dissolve: This is the human parallel of consciousness that knows all human devise. Freed from the constrictions of future and past, The Creature becomes mobile and fully functioning, no longer a patron of ersatz momentum—the vehicle that feigns movement in the guise of Progress but is as retaliating and as destructive as it advertises itself to be innovative and provocative.

Progress suppresses the individual. The ability to think through deduction eliminates all barriers. The bare recognition that all that is love proclaimed is falseness or that no good nor bad exists, except as we generate through Agreement, is an act of pure will, as providence created and was created.

Within The Creature that is human, intelligence and moveable instinct are analogous, for when the mind transits Reasoned Intent, physical adroitness and autonomic dexterity peak only at the apex of artistry. For The Creature who is whole and who has grown beyond R.I.P., there exists nothing that is impassable nor immutable. Intelligence, The Creature, is his own creator, as providence designed. The Creature that is human is master of determination and the sovereignty of will.

Judas Iscariot is well known as the betrayer of Christ. Did he betray or did he perform a volitive act as Christ taught? It was Christ's clear Intention to be put to death as an example of divine will. Judas was not his betrayer but his accomplice. The death of Jesus is unique, not as a bid for martyrdom, but as a gesture of complete submission to will. If it can be said that Jesus failed in his attempt to exemplify volition, then it must be said that his failure is the failure of mankind, for since his death, we have practiced the inverse of his teachings and we have practiced perversion of will without even the honor of shame. A crown of thorns was fitting tribute, indeed, to one who, throughout the annals of history, has been made a pestilent hand-puppet of right and good.

The divinity of will passes through zero before entering the external, temporal world. There are things that natural intelligence can see that cannot be seen through the weakened eyes of legacy. Pure intelligence is the intelligence of a child. The intelligence that we bring into the world at birth is the intelligence of the sentient. At birth, we know nothing. Our minds are open. We have no fear nor need of fear, for fear is friend. In infancy, there is no separation of being and will. As children, we walk on the paths of fear. Fear is our perfect interrogator of sense. We require no protection, and we do not know the meaning of security. We know warmth and we seek warmth. We know affection and we seek it. Now is zero to Reason. However, these things are meted out conditionally, and we are taught to accept these conditions as gratuitous documentation of Half Life. Second Voice tangibility becomes warrant.

When we look around us, what is Half Life? Have we not sold ourselves lowly in the name of love; in the name of safety? What is this false creature that we have placed in the stead of intelligence? What is the inverse of human?

Retrograde Man has armed himself to the teeth inside the grinding machinery of Reason. He shields himself in words and girds himself with declamatory weaponry. In Reason, the human inverse is ferocious and vindictive, while his designated enemy, in parallel match, is spare. Intelligence, The Creature, who lives below The R.I.P., is the parallel of original sorrow.

NOTES

NAME: DATE:

XIII

XIII

SENSES AT A LIMIT

Passive Self Blocked by Word Conscript

We are symbols, and inhabit symbols.

—Ralph Waldo Emerson

THE COMMON BOND OF IMAGINATION, hallucination and dream is expansion of the passive sense. A new limit is reached every time a boundary is crossed, even if only momentarily, in the neural pathways of the mind.

Generic fear is interrogated and removed from common failsafe or safe fear in altered state; tied to duty and pre-think analogues. With the removal of interrogated fear, we mentally engage an unknown integer that could not exist in the altered state of Paradox.

This unknown is a step away from our consignment in synthetic fear to a holistic inner Self that is charged by challenge and question. Unknown is either balanced by reprisal of logic or given over to a discovering ingenious force that is physically or mentally implemented. Sensory limit is transcended and passive memory is expanded.

What does the mind do with its discoveries? One may rationally assume that it does nothing. But this assumption is nothing other than the turning of an entrenched psyche by the hand of Reason.

The mind and heart never sleep. The old saying, "I'll sleep on it," is of merit. Information reaches the mind through the senses and resides in a kinetic cerebral mass. In its undulating movement, the mind does not rid itself of data but displaces or supplants it in storage as surrogate that has yet to be aligned by a system of checks of cause and effect. Alignment leads to final gravity, the last place that collected and recollected data goes in its descent to reach an understood or realized *a priori* match. Final gravity is the void of non-doubt within the centered Self as the mind concludes harmony with its particular slant—its particular charge.

Mental excess is imagination. Imagination, fully sensed and Reasoned, is Sixth Sense multidimensional range. Through imagination, we enter a calibrated domain—one that is adjusted to unknown realms that are possible realms when failsafed boundaries are crossed. Such a mental domain within the made subconscious does not include knowledge, process-think or logic.

Invention, whether it yields a simple wheel or the most sophisticated gadgetry of technology, requires experimentation and building of working components to assemble a working device.

Maximum sensory limit is hallucination. Extreme sensory limit is a tactile imagination or dream exploration. Conscious reality dominates, within that pallid environs of sanctioned values, a vivid waking dream that could be life. The high value accorded reality is determined by time spent with stimulus that is not a part of legacy and that is aligned with final gravity. Habitual conscious audit denotes a universally accepted axiom: Sleep is indicative of a rational fatigue.

The Self does not question what is obvious in reality—our day-to-day techniques for survival. It questions the things in our minds that are broken fragments—those things that breach our senses at a limit.

Doubt is the must-think factor—a constant reminder of Reason to feeling in a holistic Self—that is always in danger of diffusion. Introspection is emotional, and the anxiety in our inner First Voice beckons us to dream. Dreams test and stretch I synthetics and We strategies of group cohesion.

In dreams, we scan exaggerated symbolic terrains that are magnified in symbology for effect. As we climb exalted heights or plumb the recesses of an emotional landscape, we not only amplify our working roles in symbolism, but strain the mental seams to expand into passiveness: feeling as related to active prominence or Reason. If we could remain inside a dream long enough, we could undo all hypocrisy; and open ourselves to the sensitive Creature we were in pre-time.

The only moments in our lives when, without legal considerations, we may gauge sub-parallel R.I.P. without risk or consequence are within the comfortable regions of the dream. In dreams, the need for word depiction crumbles and fades to the firmness of mental and emotional resolve. Language, in active definition, becomes unnecessary because all things within the scope of dreams become symbolically enhanced and do not require the added symbology of words. In dreams, understanding of symbology is inherent and precludes the word.

Inside the walls of our Self-structured dream box, we are characters acting in serious roles. In our dreams, we are actors in a one-act play. The props are of our own design and make. Direction is at our disposal and use.

In the dream, Self is in stark control and sometimes startles the Self facade, with its inherent voice in darkness, in blunt tirades and tireless soliloquies that quell, for once, the well trained unmelodic drone of Reason.

When the information gleaned from the dream state is arbitrarily accepted as cause and effect of Reason, our emotive swellings recede and draw back into an unused surplus that must, once again, await the beckoning of the anxious voice in sleep. This settling for Half Life and slumping into vacuity is how we settle for the refuse left over from the failing to ignite the intrinsic mental fire that could warm our original Self.

It is to waste that we are born and to waste that we succumb, delivered hypoxic within a porous cerebral sink to the vortical drag of the holy mortal cesspit of excuse for Reason enacted. Reproof is left off-center. Original Self cannot automatically adjust, as is its natural wont, by decoding through emotion and the transcendence of what is now warning of incomplete and dubiously devised logical, diabolical malaise.

Reason touches off a trail of diseased warrant and charge, in lexicon, for Intention. Emotion is exempt from this pretense due to its hold on original Self in First Voice. This is a temporary letdown of interrogated information that has a dramatic effect upon active memory, causing internal noise until the mind channels its focus into avenues of release, which is comprehension by feeling. Sensitivity to all that we see, hear, taste, touch and smell bridges Self to its original emotional corridor.

In partial fact, falsified tolerance levels are violations of mental functioning. Through our arduous toil and suffering angst, we climb the desolate pinnacles of Reason, for Reason unknown, to find ourselves laced in the thin air of high altitudes, our breath spent on results for results and tomorrow's promise in future bright—for Reason and in Reason and Reason behemoth.

All suffering, and its ensuing hope for tomorrow, is false. False suffering is the guiding circle and bogus tautology of Reason pretense. As a satisfied specie, we complacently revel in the achievement of pain. We have been taught to suffer well and we pass on this legacy of false pain to our children. We are happy mutants with severed genes and split minds who do not know our place. We are made beasts of burden with false encumbrance.

We die as fakirs in glass pavilions, our every atonement sanctioned or condemned. It is the Self, unadorned in Reason and unbent, who must cast the final stone. To death we are born.

Cast into the blind end of Impasse, we are R.I.P.P.E.D.! The substance of our lives is sucked down into the bare regions below culture and means. We exist for designated function only. We have no matched reciprocation to Self: When we come to face a mirror, we see fragments—the disunion of man and beast.

As a sapient specie, we are apart and adrift. Our rule is our madness. Murderers have no friends.

We are dutifully bound in knowledge that is the prerequisite prison of our own devise. We set aside the original working Self in favor of what we take for granted, and to which we swear allegiance in the name of duty, as demonstrated reality extracted from Reason.

What can we know of life when we intentionally elect to live in a box? What can we know when we do not dare to leave our cells even when the doors are left open? We are quite safe inside the cubicle of results for results and jobs for jobs.

We say, "Better safe than to ever hear the dogs."

Indeed: Better to cloak ourselves in ignorance than to ever admit our culpability. We disavow ourselves through synthetic guilt and we wallow in our Blame and Blame worth. As a poor excuse for a specie of being, we are slovenly and biased and vain. Arrogance is our pale taper, and we have used its light for guidance for centuries; we burrow through our nasty, darkened paths through the oblique dirt of science and government and religion and in our arrogance, we know nothing. Frenzied rodents annihilate themselves.

Sub-parallel teachings dictate original Self-annihilation through the arrogance of complacence. We trade Feeling for sacrosanct blessing and the rewards for not having to Feel. We submit to anything and everything in the name of Entity or Deity. Within original Self, we have no shame, and yet in Half Life, we are required to prostrate ourselves before all monoliths of business and commerce that are accomplished for original Self-annihilation in favor of group cohesion.

Justification for the dumping of casualties of Half Life into a common grave is power for strategic advantage. We are so adept at Self-murder and so cunning in Self-deceit that we kill with utmost precision and in utter disregard.

Indeed, the human credo could be, "There is no disregard

like the present disregard."

Duty forged from Blame is senses at a limit. The limit is at a point that is directly below The R.I.P. in the human psyche, just inside the parameters of the Self facade.

Sensory limits are only limited until Entity structure falters. In structural breakdown, the downloading of human parody begins.

In the civilized age, this involves degeneration of the human being by bands or groups who fortify themselves through acquisition of loyalty to the august speculation that future reward is at hand; that spoils may be taken. In times of confusion and strife, group-appointed or made-holy and made-sapient zealots of Reason fashion a kind of sacrilegious faith, in pretense to religion, through the abandonment of Self and First Voice and through wanton hatred of the human Creature and with the beatitude of opportune adversity, using Blame Loop to full advantage.

The R.I.P. is a treasure trove of fortune and fame for those cunning enough to ravage such a handed-down horn of plenty: the riches made from the duty of We. There is much money to be made from Blame by proxy and enough hirelings to do the dirty work. A bludgeoning master race requires the blind obedience of submissive adjutants and sentries.

Such incremental duty to Entity is rough parody of all that is carefully hidden in Half Life—that which could be but is not— and held in vast emptiness that awaits but the "twinkling of an eye" and the transport of change.

Until such change, the rector of Reason will be the hangman with his killing knot, and enough is never enough upon the makeshift mental scaffolds that lie beyond the jagged cerebral edges of The R.I.P. toward the dismal parameters and barren borders of the senses at a limit.

Before there was Agreement and before knowledge became enactment, the senses of the human being were open. He knew original Self. There was no Reason in keeping. The human being had no wily need for what may be described as two hearts: one man made in determination and filled not with substance, but pretense; the other, unknown but transparent and fluid in dimensional acumen.

The sense of original Self had no rhyme nor Reason and was naturally pushed to an emotional edge. Sensory actions and reactions were not intellectually organized and predestined as they are within the Paradox of civilized man. Emotions, as cause and effect of sensory stimulus, were easily recognized and imparted.

To paraphrase an old maxim, man, in original Self, did not "look a gift horse in the mouth" as his civilized and cultivated made prototype has been taught to do. Original Self of man accepted both his vices and virtues with never a thought of what could be right or wrong. His actions were without ruse. The human being, in original Self, was Self-adjusting.

What was harmful to others immediately became punishment of the Self. Pain inflicted became pain sustained; no penal code necessary. In essence, the human being has no need of law.

In the flight from sensual awareness that has occurred and that will occur in the late nineteenth, twentieth and twenty-first centuries, the sensitivity of mankind is at a standstill and is in sub-parallel shock. Religion and politics, fanaticism on many fronts, and a driving need to subdue and to be subdued are the "opiates of the masses." Symbolic overload creates a mental substate of suspended animation that, in its stagnation, grinds upon itself. We live inside a rogue mental state that is unbalanced in its helter-skelter of noun-verb application.

Action stimulus does not belong to feeling but to Reason. Reason is the unifying hold of Intention and the Reason word or charge of motive. Motive is the modus operandi of senses at a limit; and its underlying logos; and pure, sapient cause. The grand effect of such ballyhoo of degenerative warrant is Intention and present disregard for the perfect Now that resides in original Self.

Legally, the human being is kept within limits. Law is testament and proof of Half Life boundary. Law and its Reason is insolent and disdainful of the human being and its original Self essence.

Law, within a tight circle of Reason and Blame Loop, makes of the proud sapient specie a race of flagellants and scourgers who bow, like curs, at the whipping post, all the while lapping at the hard boots of an unlimited authoritarian master that is Reason.

This is the picture of the sublime height to which we climb, ever hopeful and dutiful, for resultant end jobs with its top prize and top seated authority to Blame.

When we consider authority to Blame, we must inspect the seriousness of belief—that which is made consequential—and made truth. We accept, in blind faith and trust, what is allotted to us as guarantee. But what value is guarantee when redemption is fraud? As creatures born into The R.I.P of latter-day earth, what other can we afford to believe?

It is belief that gives glory to thugs and misusers. It is belief that allows for starvation and genocide. It is our sucking, swallowing-into-hollowness dire need to believe that consumes us. Belief is our alpha and omega: our beginning and end. In diaphanous pity and in immeasurable shame, en masse, it is I to We to They that forms the circular emblematic shape of the serpent who swallows his own tail.

Lacking and hollow within ourselves, we elect and assign authority to Blame. In this manner, we believe ourselves Blameless. In this manner, we consider ourselves absolved. But, in the Paradox of The R.I.P., we disown and degrade through the pretense of guilt as though we could be worthy of it. We are unworthy of guilt.

The muscle brain approach of Paradox upon the human being is a forced mental entry—a breach in the universal parallel of mind/body continuum. We hear the fair prattle and chatter of process-think from cradle to the grave. We learn to speak it before we can walk; our unfettered child's mind filling up and becoming stymied with word symbols that are the blocks and barricades to our senses.

The regions of the mind that are beyond the set sensual limits are stripped of influence and have no voice. Mind and body are kept at odds, the Reasons implanted in active memory for use, until contention between Reason and feeling builds to the limit of usable motive. Reason, then, given to caprice, reverses polarity to all that is Reasonable to feel; it cannot entice its heretofore willing victim into the false suffering and quasi-grief that attends the inability to use Reason for Reason.

Sensual limits are discharged when the mind/body constant begins the purging and decoding of seeded symbolic blocks. Such unraveling is the breakdown or falling through to the original Self and begins a devolution until end becomes the beginning—until Half Life becomes the simplified reality of sensual completion. Through the introspection of passive memory that was once held at bay by active Intention and speculative Reason, as Agreed and permitted, the falling through to I abandonment is realized.

When we mentally digest data, the churning of the senses is not based on Agreement but is forced into such flat-line focus by symbolic use of the verbal and written word. Though only superficially connected to the five senses through denotation and connotation—messages implied and specified—such charge appeals to sound and sight. Reason taints sight and sound by oversimplification. Our mental agility and access to First Voice is blurred and lost.

Sight in Reason teaches lessons in purblind truth, while Reasoned sound imparts decerebration. By so doing, mock Agreement is made that stimulates Reason by Intention to do so but fails in that to do so only means to mean or to make meaning to do so. Backward and forward, word symbolic motive in Reasoned slick is out to match consequence but defers to what is of no consequence and the synthetic as replaceable real. To do so, we are practitioners and auditors of an artful and ancient hindbrain creed of stone cold animosity that is devoted to We context and tribal warp. Our congenital fissure of covetous Impasse and Paradoxical facade of Self, makes of us the prodigal scions to a race of prey—a tradition of man stalked by future past and cowed into servility by the enormity of its ignorance of a redemptive Now. We are enslaved by trepidation and horror at the very contingency of our own sentient skinlessness. As menial subjects of Reason who gird ourselves with false pride and false angst, we are haughty victims in desperate search for an enemy.

Our most sapient and superior assumption to will is a most angular and reedy disregard.

Punctiliousness to autonomically imposed information sets us dutiful to sub-parallel motion. Its speed beguiles us with its pulling tow that draws even our most basic sensuality into a flatline of Agreement. We assail the sense of touch and make of it hypocrisy and fraud, even make of it something vile and squalid. It is as a dastardly race of prey that we pick and glean from a fallen-through corpus of Reason to savor a fair swill that we reckon to be good and evil.

The irony is that the more that we designate evil as that which is unwanted, while stalking the good in order to own and possess and command, the more evil comes of it. The mockery of Reason is the spectacle of the most upright of vertebrate beasts, with a specialized and enchanting cerebrum, who wallows in his own misery and thrives on the favors of adversity.

As the most intrinsically meek creatures on earth, we do not need Agreement to guarantee our gentleness; to know tenderness and caring without condition. Within original Self human, mildness precludes and succeeds condition. Agreement annuls what could be like love and obliterates it. Agreed love is a parsimonious payment for position in Entity, however grand or meager.

By the year 2000, the percentage of people who are actually producing goods will fall to less than thirty percent of sub-parallel. Seventy percent will be in the business of pushing and enforcing symbols. The business of zero marketing is much larger than the production of goods or the future production of goods. Automated consumption, via the accelerated speed of The R.I.P., will consume us, and we will be both its wily accomplices and willing victims.

The outer banks of the absurd and the insane will become a third parallel of fantasy, and tolerance levels will be violated. The current desperation will be replaced by exhaustion. Drugs, both those that are chemically induced and the drug of media, will control the instincts of the decrepit and bedraggled masses.

All for the sake of a failed method of Reason, wrought from failed Intentions and failed motives.

All of us for the ultimate hypocrisy of good versus evil and the legal travail.

Senses at a limit: R.I.P.

Addendum

In legal parlance, motive is the moving force or power which impels to action for a definite result. Intent is the purpose to use a particular means to effect such result: These definitions are cited in *People versus Weiss; app. Div. 463, 300 W.Y.S. 249-255* In this authorized definition of Intention, we can see that impetus is construed as an act of Reason. Further, in *Parks versus Bartlett 236 Mich. 460, 210, N.W. 492, 494, 47, ALR 1128,* the faculty of Reason is described as what is rational and governed by Reason; under the influence of Reason and Agreeable to Reason. In *Clausen versus state, 21 Wyo., 505, 133, p. 1055, 1056,* the legal conclusion is an Entity authorized enclosure that ordains think process within narrow confines of appropriate parameters.

N O T E S

NAME: DATE:

NOTES

NAME: DATE:

XIV

——XIV——

COMPROMISE

The Share in Blame Loop Synthesis

Something was dead in each of us,
And what was dead was Hope.

—from *The Ballad of Reading Gaol*
Oscar Wilde

COMPROMISE IS THE EXCHANGE OF ONE IDEA FOR ANOTHER. We seek efficacious results through compromise, and compromise, with its desirable and predictable outcome, is pretense and hypocrisy. Compromise is irony. There is no one more cynical than on who negotiates compromise through bargain and rapprochement. Truce is disagreement pacified and beguiled. Truce is bought hate.

Education is the bondsman's compromise. All slaves to Agreement are educated. Education is the trademark of our indenture to Reason. We train to become efficacious and deceiving. We are trained in artfulness. By the constraint of civilization, we Agree to become less than the essence of our being. The will to Agree makes of us skillful solicitors of colloidal happiness and smooth disregard. It is through the compromise of education that we live placidly in future past. By far, it is the educated slave who prostrates himself most gratuitously before the mastered hands of time, and he does so for Reason, and to Reason good, by doing so.

Who stands to benefit from Reason more than those highly trained in lexicon and technique of appeasement? A well-trained cretin has no purpose except the purpose of his purposelessness and his qualified capacity to justify. Words, in Reason slick, justify and validate. A cultured buffoon is free to be a buffoon and a well-paid one as long as he can authenticate, through jargon, his purposeful lack of purpose.

Modern corporate conglomerates employ large numbers of the drear Agreed in apparent hope of attracting others of this strain into the commercial fold. Those who possess developed skill or who have attained a specialized craft and who have clear and designated purpose are retained as underlings to serve those who are without purpose. Highly skilled technicians are prized as chattel for purpose and as vassals for affirmation. The drear Agreed are continually shuffled around from post to post, without loss or dread of loss, while the purposefully skilled work always under the threat of removal.

In future past, there is no such thing as real manufacture. In future past, through the slick purposelessness of purpose, we reside in ersatz momentum—the truth-telling lie; the false value of time. Production is surreptitious and plethoric, nearly accidental, and always reported as debauchery. In ersatz momentum, real manufacture or production is unwarranted: To gain is to lose. We receive credit only by discredit. All value is valueless.

In this world of compromise and remunerated Reason for compromise and devaluation, one could be God and still be R.I.P.P.E.D.! In the made-meant-mean realm of results for results, the introspective concept of God is discredited. Beyond money, there is no God. What do we revere? Indeed, what else besides money is worthy of reverence? Money and the meaning of money are the only things that Retrograde Man of Reason has not debased! Wealth is envied but never Blamed, not even by those who are less wealthy or those who are poor. The poor man balks at the fortunes of the rich, but, given the chance to trade places with the wealthy man, he would do so without hesitation. Gambling against all the odds is a poor man's compromise.

Compromise is verification of purposelessness and Agreement to fail. We fail by compromise and by the collective will to misery. Misery is, by inversion, the promise and hope for amity. The hope of amity is a magnet, and once drawn to it, its devotees seemingly cannot let go. And with the promise of amity, its devotees validate and perpetuate misery. The human condition of misery is bred, and we crave it and seek it and give it credence by name, and we name it pleasure. Pleasure is a myth. Misery is made real.

Supplication to the promise of amity is the fundamental lesson in subjugation and the will to government. We could govern ourselves and have pleasure as it exists in the constant of Now, in recondite awareness of Self. But we abandon and refuse in order to delegate and solicit, always, promise.

To be always on the edge of sadness is to know joy, for joy is occult and concealed and it is concealed for Reason. Stoked on false dreams, we seek love when love is Now. Filled with false hope, we seek relief when relief is Now. The human being is hunted and is hunting when Now, the hunt is finished. We can have no need that cannot be filled. We can have no sorrow.

At the point that sorrow and joy condense is the point that the parallel of life becomes complete. Until parallel match, the human being is a thing disjoined, and the parallel of his separation into eternal separation is The R.I.P. We separate our feeling from the integrity to feel as we are taught the legacy of The R.I.P.: Replace feeling with exegesis. We feel but we mold feeling to fit word matrix. We warrant our feeling into what we know to be Agreeable. We compromise.

Agreement to fail is failure to define. We react to Reason without question. We obey. Through contrition, we gain the right to Blame

Dignity repels obedience to compromise. When the human being, in Disagreement, disallows compromise, he finds capacity and original will that is pristine and beyond reproach. One who, through introspection of critical thought, can defy Reason and give homage to the will to Self through disparity and definition becomes both creator and creation. One who, through crit-

ical thought, begins to understand creation, finds dignity that is
the parallel of providence. The human being, only through the
selection of will, excels. It is through the creation of the Self
that the bondsman is freed. Given the choice of the splendors
of freedom or the flat continuation of drudgery, what can we
choose? What do we choose?

Indifference atones restraint. We compromise.

Prestige is the gift of hypocrisy to the hypocrites of Reason
pretense. The slave unchained does not seek prestige. In Self-
creation, he does not need Agreement. The bondsman who has
been freed is Self-made. His dignity is a wealth beyond prestige.
He has no barriers. Reason is not his cross to bear.

The man who was called Jesus Christ set his example of
divine will two thousand years ago. Have we learned nothing
from his will to variance?

We split and punish. We obey and crush. We repent of the
splendors of Self and find no dishonor. We are unworthy of
shame.

The promise of good is the ultimate hoax. How can there be
good in the dishonor of the most gentle and caring creature on
earth? We exhort morality when we are most immoral. We vote
for honesty when we are most dishonest, and we expect love
when we cannot define it—only pretend it for Reason. In Half
Life, we merit nothing beyond the certitude of depravity because
we crave it. We merit nothing beyond degradation because we
want it. We are not loved because we are incapable of love.

Control is need, even in parody. We ape and we mimic for
Reason. We are controlled by fear, when fear is our most free-
ing beauty. As hypocrites, we stand to lose if we relinquish control and relinquish the power of control; relinquish the empowered symbology of those appointed to control.

To live beyond control means that there could be no such
thing as Reason nor its inversions, Reason fantastic and criminality. Beyond control, religion and politics would no longer be
tolerated. The human being, in Self-government beyond con-

trol, would adjust according to its needs. World population would decrease and anguish would diminish as human need fulfilled human need. Beyond control, the human being could adjust and deliver. Creation and genius, no longer homogenized into right to know and right to produce, could function fully, without value or virtue. Creation could realize fear naturally and without the synthesis of fear. Genius and productivity could become common occurrences and offerings in timelessness. Beyond control, goodness could have no reward.

Without reward and without punishment, good and evil are antiquated. Ersatz momentum could cease and its destruction.

The provision of good is subjugation. To compromise in the name of good is to submit and join ranks with those who have perfected servitude. There is no such thing as evil, because evil is good as long as most Agree. Crime, within the context of good, is desired and encouraged. Without the provision of good, murderers would be murdered without exemption: The human being is Self-adjusting.

The double fantasies of law and lawlessness drive a wedge of illogic in the human psyche. We believe in justice as crusade. What is a criminal except the image of cowardice? The logic of good is that good cannot condone evil. The illogic of good is that good promotes evil and craves it. We live in a split: All thieves are good and honor is defiled. The archaic concept of good is enriched by the equally outmoded concept of evil. Law has no bearing except as prevaricator for good. Upholders of law are impostors of justice who revile their humanity.

In life below The R.I.P., there is no law. Law, in its mockery of purity, favors invincibility in the form of money: Law is currency and God is currency. There is no greater perfection in the sovereignty of humankind than the law and the holy unction of currency.

The idea of disorder assumes that there is order when there is none except the order of ruse. Order made and enforced is pathology. The rudiments of order are things. Control cannot hold. Disorder is abdication to things.

Enforcers of law know this well. There is no such thing as crowd control: Those who endeavor to hold back a mob become a part of the mob. Rulers are ruled. There is no one who can vanquish who will not be vanquished. The notion of a ruling class is nonsense. There can be no need for social revolution because aristocrats destroy themselves by their dependence on sycophants who, as necessary parasites, weaken by their burdensome demands and by their willingness to perform life as duty as a proven method to buy time. This is the symbiosis of the rich and the poor. There has always been interest in chronicling of the mythical underclass.

We are idolaters of allegory and parable—stories of heroes and villains, princes and paupers; innocence and arrogance. The idle rich mimic the idle poor. Time is worthless and abridged, and its seeming lack of value is its consigned virtue by Agreement. There is no class struggle but a struggle for time; because time is the currency that buys life. Elimination of time is elimination of partition and alienation. Outside time, there is no compromise.

Communism failed in its refusal to recognize the inductive needs of the rich for the poor and the poor for the rich: Denizens of the working class have no desire to rule except through rule by subjugation. Otherwise, the denizens of the working class would make their way from the working class. This is the major premise of capitalism. However, capitalism fails in its sanctimonious and false defense of one political-economic class while clearly favoring the other and still failing to recognize symbiosis and bind. In Paradox, the ruling class is the confederated class. Paradox creates the autocratic poor and the underprivileged rich. Thievery on both sides is postulated and fostered.

Any form of political revolution has an inchworm effect: Little new ground is covered, and its significance is measured by cause. To say that history is the history of class struggle is beside the point. Only one accustomed to some degree of inherited comfort and financial legacy could argue that. What we call history is the history of belief inversion. Except as construed and manipulated by law, there is no class struggle. Groups rise and avenge. Hearkened by The Voice of It, we take sides and Reason dictates. War is the tool of Reason and ultimate compromise.

Issues of race and class are brandished and used by law as means to ends. Innocence and guilt are insignificant. Political right is the culprit's best friend. The facade of law shrivels in the face of good undone for good. Justice served is injustice pardoned. In lawful Paradox, the substance of humanity has no due: It is compromised. In the fair name of God, The Certificate, any debauchery of reflected distortion can be made equitable for the parallel of justice.

Prestige is the last false gift from a last false god. What is creativity and what is genius when faced with the promise of compromise? Is it not more beneficial to succumb than to surpass? The fantastic shaft of compromise collects its human property more by its enormity and its insuperable impassiveness than by consummation or fulfillment. Promise is enough to buy promise. Sanction is the same as deed. As long as the wants and needs of humanity are authorized, we can find no need to doubt, for doubt is the seed of change. Variance defies time, and time is the keeper of promise. The more that we doubt, the less that we are compromised. One who has extended himself beyond time has no fear, because fear is friend. Outside time, Intelligence is The Creature, and The Creature will not tolerate false verdict nor will to suffer. The will to matter is the will to sentient expansion.

Definition does not exist for those in pursuit of control over meaning and meaning is implied. Values are implied through legacy and group ideal. Connotation and denotation are meaning manufactured for Reason. Made meaning assures the failure of The Creature in R.I.P. We are all deemed worthy or made guilty by virtue of implication. Worthiness to false value makes of us slaves. Guilt, when we are synthetically made worthy of it, is utter destruction. Chaos is the fury of the immaculate unjust, who live inside fortified right and who rectify by made fear.

Silence is the touch of the hand that asks and the look of the eyes that seek. Silence cannot be made, nor can it be balanced nor made equivocal. Silence has no parallel and no inversion. Silence, like creation and variance, is ultimate adoration. There is no greater recourse that can be called love.

When we can realize that what we want is what we cannot possess, we can live within the soft emptiness of silence.

The negative of hope is not despair. Silence, without hope, is life without pacification. To live beyond hope is a pilgrimage to the heart: As the petals of a flower fall away, so do the intrigues of the mind. Is the perfect heart unadorned, a thing to be reviled? How can we consider that which is without hope as less than perfect hope? How is it that we can induce the positive but cannot deduce at all?

Why is Why a trick question? Why is a ruse because we will not traverse the negative. Half Life is dull and gray but with a colorfully enticing facade. We trade our senses for acceptance, and this is compromise. Credibility is failure by indenturement.

The human being, in Paradox, has been R.I.P.P.E.D. threadbare and made inconsiderable. We want for nothing and yet make of ourselves supplicants. We accept requisition as truth. In Paradox, there is no truth beyond Reason. In Reason/Impasse, all truth is mendacity. By our own invention, we resemble our shame, which is our weakness.

The end of time is Now. The sorrow of The Creature has no magistrate. The end of time is the genesis of creation.

When we can deduce the negative into the positive; when we can learn to live without inverse reciprocation and can accept all that is carefully denied, we will have learned to live without applied meaning. Life without meaning appliqué is sensorial Impassionment. Life without cosmetic meaning is joy.

The human being is born into a paradise of expectation.

Affliction, within the altered state of our living death, is ready-made sin and sacrosanct Blame: Torment, from the dark moment of our birth, is blessed.

The pity of Reason is the only Reason for Pity, and shame, when we are made worthy, is proof. Variance, without indemnity, is the sapient will to a hope inferno. Disparity and the vigor of juxtaposition is life. Life that is vehement requires no proof. That which crawls and moves and hears and sees needs no affidavit.

NOTES

NAME: DATE:

NOTES

NAME: DATE:

XV

─────── XV ───────

CONVERTIBLE SENSE

Reverse Hypocrisy: The Prize

No path leads from a knowledge of
that which is to that which should be.

—Albert Einstein

THE INTENDED AND ABSURD NOTION, first of all, in lexicon, that
a thing called a sense exists, precludes and dismisses any chance
of understanding even the possibility of sensing. Within lexicon
and within the constricts of Provoker Function, sensory perception is controlled and relegated to Reason. From early childhood, we are taught to place trust in words and implication.
The meanings of words are conveyed most succinctly by actions,
and these actions are forthrightly opposed to what their word
meanings purport to mean.

Young children are especially sensitive to the manners by
which words are inverted in the minds of their elders. Children
are keen in their observations of adult hypocrisy and absolute
fabrication. We teach them, very early, the concept of trust. We
teach them to trust so that we may further indoctrinate them
with the legacy of hypocrisy and duplicity. The first step in
learning the craft of cunning is learning to trust. One can only
learn to deceive when one can fully trust because it is with
moral deceit that one instills trust. Trust is ultimate deceit and
ultimate cunning.

Can we recall what was in our childish minds the first time a
parent told us that we must hold his hand when we crossed a

street? Did we not question and wonder? Is it not a hypocrisy that we teach our children, by our own sullen belief in compromise, that there is such a thing as safety when they can be killed simply by walking? We avow safety and empower the figment and article of fear, while yet we scorn and shrink from the lessons of fear that can have no guile!

Satisfaction makes us soft and miserly. We console ourselves that our pity is our compassion, but how ruthlessly does our pity, concealed as compassion, designate and condemn! Is it with pity that we maim and disfigure for progressive design? What bravery of compassion imbues us with the mettle for war? What bravery of compassion moves us to don the proud fashions of conflict? Does pity beget tyranny?

Compassion is bigoted, and in Blame Loop, compassion is Agreed contempt.

For what do we vote, and to what do we pray? What are the dictates of policy and religion if not malignancy of Self. Is Self-annihilation the passed down and preordained legacy of man?

Policy and belief are the invectives by reproof that give absolution to Retrograde Man.

If there is honor in guilt, then we are untainted.

Hypocrisy, by necessity, is a worthy aphrodisiac! How arrogant are we to believe emphatically in the excellence and value of the world that we have made and to trust in it so well that we, by conjoint and conscripted will, conceive and give birth!

Every birth signifies the perpetuation of fraud. Every birth is the birth of untruth. Every infant is burdened by his parent with the legacy of despair. Every child is numbered and held accountable from birth. Every child is a commercial product; a consumer to be consumed; a profit margin and a new host for rule by parasite.

Every child pays dearly for his conception. In Paradox of The R.I.P., proof is reproof.

The viper, as symbol of repentance, becomes our point of prestige. We relegate all misery to sin, when sin is the willing perpetuation of misery. If such a thing could exist as Satan, then he is the Great Accountant. What could be evil except as we enumerate?

Birth, as an instance of truth as untruth, is the progenitor of consequence. How can there be such a creature as the happy baby when even the fact of his birth is a fabrication? We fabricate the birth of life by relegation and number. Facts are Agreed falsifications. We certify birth with numeration of facts that mean nothing outside Agreement.

History is the enumeration of the scarring effects of Reason; and history is the quagmire of atonement; though our atonement does not resolve; but builds; and has its own momentum within the circle of Blame. For legacy, we condemn and condemn again and are, ourselves, condemned.

History as atonement has no bearing on Self because its Reason is forgotten even as the residuals of it remain. History is a snare of time ordering, and it is time's rote promise.

As long as we Agree to live in time, history will repeat. When we can live outside the barrier of time, in timelessness, we can discover that what we once Agreed to be time is the memory of time in circumstances of Blame and storage of facts in time.

Removed from time, one finds that one must exert his natural will and accomplish, for endeavor outside the wall of time is the beginning of Resolve.

There is not one single act of volition contained within the constricts of time. Inside time, the human being is a drone: a worker insect in a contemptible hive. Though he dutifully makes busy, he resents the cause of his busyness, for below The R.I.P., he recognizes this impetus as force, and even as he recognizes Reason for force, he mentally demurs as he outwardly continues. The human drone subjects himself to the muscle brain of push and shove commerce, and he works for Intention to succeed or to force interpretation. What succeeds by force is a progression of formatted think-process that serves as the joint for propagation of future to future tense or usable nouns to usable verbs.

Purity is unacceptable. A society bred on placation and dissimulation cannot accept purity. We coax and bribe and coerce our children from their purity. The purity of children is that they will not be contained. Children sense quickly, and they move on quickly: They refuse singularity of method for the completeness of freedom.

Systematically, we teach our children what may be called the law of the sepulcher. We impart to them the quietness of the grave. We teach them to be quiet and we teach them to accept boredom; we expect them to be excellent in their boredom and excellent in their misery of inheritance.

We are pleased with our children when they are most like us. We are happy with our children when they have mastered our contrivances and Agree to the perpetuation of sanctimony.

What honor and what strength is there in the mastering of perfect mediocrity? What strength is there in mastering perfect ineptness? There is no strength and no will and no conviction in perfect Paradox.

By Agreement, we dilute. The master race is mastered. We are a generation of slaves and the producers of slaves. Repentance of the Self is our handed-down legacy of Self-hate.

The convertible sense is our altered state. What we claim to see and to know may be exactly what we do not see and do not know. The seeing of it has already been bought and sold—and bought again. In Reason, we bargain for what we see and hear because we must, or we will be told and it will be enforced— that what we see and hear is imagination.

If what we see and hear is not Agreed, then we will deny our senses. The denial of the senses is the basis of Half Life in Altered State. We live our lives in the fogged existence of the terrible tomorrow. There can be no such thing as happiness because what could be like happiness is squandered in promise, and promise has no temperance and no mercy.

Trapped within the promise of future past, The Creature called human is contorted and warped.

Within the cramped confines of time, there are no human beings: What have we become?

Retrograde is poisoned by the stagnating pools of his inversions. Reciprocals tumble and fall, yet we do deny their demise and continue to build them, despite their vacuity, through Reason until all meaning that can be reciprocated fails. What is left to us is Reason inverted, and Reason inverted is the tool of our devastation.

To intentionally fall so far from Reason, when Reason has long been our common virtue and our common motive, will be our last fall. Volition has no surrogate but Reason, and the charge of Reason has grown weak.

As words fail, belief breaks down: What was once sold as hope becomes despair. What was once touted as faith becomes faithlessness. Stripped of Reason, the human being, in his nakedness, longs to protect what is intrinsically most beautiful. The human being, unmasked, is splendid in his bareness, yet longs for concealment and is afraid.

Progress and time convert the living senses into hardened barriers to the Self—that is Intelligence, The Creature—that is the being undone. Feeling inverted and hardened to specific Reason is made commerce. Job focus leaves us devoid of feeling because feeling is discouraged as it is exploited. We do not love so such as we are taught to love. We do not love but are sold the idea of loving, and we bargain for it and control for it and are controlled by it. Rather than to share in the joy of Self, we select the split, for we seek to revere The R.I.P. and its artificial fragmentation. We rejoice in our breach of consciousness and revel in its disquiet as a substitution for life when there is no life but existence, which we make and supplant with Half Life and infuse it with the noise of our ignorance—our refusal.

Like members of an audience in an old-time medicine show, we want to believe the fantastic and will not discern sincerity from hollowness. We believe in remedies and fixes that are swindles and dodges. There is no quick remedy for the malady of The R.I.P.

Our duty is to the lie and the lie is our duty. We claim knowledge as right to plunder, and our faculties of sight and sound are our weaponry in altered state—our functional convertible sense.

Glory is our misdeed. Wealth is honor no matter how dishonorable is method. There is not good and evil, because evil is good as long as it is determined.

If, as the Bible of Christianity states, there comes a time that the meek shall inherit the earth, then the meek shall not be the meek, but shall be the integral human being, whole and intact, and with consummate will unparalleled by Reason.

From interrogative transit through Self is found majesty of will which is will to zero. The integral Self is boundless. In life below The R.I.P., will is done. The will to Self is change that is not capricious, and change is the key to zero space

Change is immutable and constant. Its velocity does not vary. Change is not projected momentum by false impetus, but is dissolution. Resolve is that which changes imperceptibly; is subtle and without rancor or voice; and without visual rebuke. Change needs no proof.

Through will to Self, there can be no need to live inside the citadel of controlled fear. Barriers crumble. To behold the man stripped of Reason and falsity of feeling is to behold light that is immersed in voiceless and sightless astonishment.

Contrition that is sheepishness makes of us lesser things. The mammon on which we feed is token goodness and failsafe to horror.

The splendor that we miss is our sadness. The mythic grace of the fragile mortal has not been known. When we can touch without breaking, and when we can bend without deforming, the inversion of truth can be known.

There is no present like the present and there is no tomorrow that cannot be today.

NOTES

NAME:

DATE:

N O T E S

NAME: DATE:

—— XVI ——

IMPORTANCES

Assets in Grim Impartiality

When everyone is somebody,
then no one's anybody.

—W. S. Gilbert

THAT WHICH IS IMPORTANT WAS ONCE ACCEPTED AS UNIMPORTANT, and that which is unimportant will not be important.

Obviously, there is nothing that can be important until we are removed from altered state and into the realm of Self that can regard fear. In Self regard, the ability to Reason is the ability to not Reason, because all Reason is pretense. Pretense to Reason is avoidance of feeling at all costs. So Reason, despite its claim to logic and to knowledge, is not Reason, because it ignores Self in regard of Self.

How can something which claims to be ultimate Reason ignore vast regions that no one, when pressed, can deny exist? Is it Reasonable to ignore what is evident and clear?

The mass mind of Paradox in R.I.P. cuts off from that which could be clear. Reason pretense discounts human feeling in favor of rational bondage, and by so doing is known as Reason. To split or divide the senses into R.I.P. is to favor outcome that is not Reason enough to be Reason.

It is Reasonable to expect that a man should strap himself to a yoke and to toil until his dying breath in favor of that which he cannot understand and cannot obtain, and it is Reasonable to expect that a man shall profess belief in that which his nature

questions. It is Reasonable to expect that a man will give up freedom in favor of constraint. It is Reasonable to expect that the
human being will do this because he has done so.

We must ask: What holds us? What tethers us to our restraints?
We do what we despise in order to earn what we despise: What
we despise is important.

We despise the conveyor that pushes us, and yet, for Reason,
we will not let it go. We reinforce our legacy of slavery in our
children and we hand it down. We do not teach our children to
think, but we teach them to obey, and we do so because we
hold artificial belief that all that we teach them is right.

What if there was a child who refused. What if there was one
child who said, "No, I will not," and what if that child made his
own way; took matters upon himself in such a way that, by his act,
he could show us that there is no tender mercy that can be met
with mercy until all Reason pretense, so carefully taught, falls?

What if this child studied knowledge but did not sell it? What
if this child understood Reason to feeling and acted upon his
understanding? What if this child knew fear as his friend and
had no fear? What if he knew the silence that lives inside him?

Would we stop him? Would we impose upon him harsh penal-
ties? Would we rob him of his life precisely because he knows life?

When we make of value and virtue the importances of life,
would stopping him become a thing of utter importance? When
does murder become right, and how do we murder righteously
and judiciously? We take away life, piece by piece, studiously
and assiduously. Murder by piecemeal is commonplace and it is
justified. It is done for love, and it is done for obedience, and it
is done in the fair names of education and medicine and law
and all industrialized swindle. Does technology improve people
or make them more accepting of rule by technology?

When, exactly, do the perpetrators of Reason pretense themselves begin to unravel? From cradle to the grave, we are indoctrinated with the seeds of our extinction. As soon as we learn to
crawl, we are expected to learn to walk. As soon as we learn to

talk, we are expected to comply. As soon as we comply, we are expected to initiate.

Is it not fitting that the young live long enough to see their masters die? Those who have taught us well that Reason is our master will, by the dissolution of their bodies, realize the will to fatality and defy their own value as their flesh starts to crumble. Do we learn anything from the lessons of death? What worth is Reason pretense if it is disproved by mortality? What is the final prank played upon the living by the dead?

Life, as we know it, is a hoax. From cradle to grave, we are bought and sold.

Nothing is important.

Truth as we know it is made confident by Agreed intent. Confidence affirms belief. Affirmed belief is pronouncement of membership. There is no other truth but confidence.

Facts are contrived by Intention. If the human mind is afraid, it should be afraid, because we live in a world that is distant and remote from The Creature in remedial wholeness.

What we have made of the human being is a thing that is gnarled and twisted and bent up that once was erect and perfect and without misery.

We have ample Reason to shrink from this damaged aspect of ourselves. We are our opposition and the mirrored reflection of the convertible human creature. The human inverse has become grotesque in its ideals and absolutes. Its solutions are monstrous and its pretense fantastic as it moves toward an ever widening fissure—the split into which we must fall; the breach in the human parallel of consciousness; our blind end unto end; appendix to tomorrow; perpendicular reality: Flatness is protocol inside The R.I.P.

The door to the mind is putrescent and abortive, shut off by legacy and by coercion to duty. The mind is airless. The sub-parallel of Reason pretense is out of time, out of Progress, and out of promise.

Yet there are a few happy people. All those who profess hap-

piness do so from the necessity of fear in duty unless they are
above fear and duty, and if they are above it, then they have full
use of lexicon for empowerment and right to happiness.
Through proper use of Blame, they are the subscribers and
issuers of The Word. They know language and they have license
to use. Those empowered by lexicon know material happiness
and they have no want except right to want.

Knowledge is bankrupt. License to speak is unobtainable to
the minions, and those who claim to speak for them have
become smug, and though suspicious, are not suspected. The
masses do not trust their political and religious leaders, but mis-
trust in the race to have is unimportant. Few people are fully
aware of those who lead them.

Political failsafe is a mockery of humanity for the empowered
unknown who are elected to enact misery.

The regal unpoor cast no vote, and the poor unrich have no
need. The pressing of a lever in a booth is a desperate act by
those who must lose. There is no life in the middle. For those
who desperately cling to the middle, the failure of their Agreement is their only affirmation. A vote to win is as good as a vote
to lose. Politicians are credited by their discredit, and they are
masters of the credit/discredit game and party to the circle of
Blame. Every vote for is a vote against in the circle of Blame.

Importances are defined by time, and time is made by those
who are credited in time. Production and purpose are time:
There are no products that are timeless. Merit is based on time
in terms of word slick. What is valued is Reason given that can
be qualified by Reason spoken.

Nothing is real. Sincerity, in timed confidence, is a scam.

We must ask: In timed R.I.P., what is gained but the falsity of
momentum? In truth as we know it, do we not all reel from the
motion? In ersatz momentum, does it not feel as if we are
embarked on a fast journey to desolation? How must it feel to
stop? How must it feel to slow down? Can we dare?

If we want to stop our destruction, we must stop our rush

toward it. Is it difficult to imagine a world without speed? How fast is Blame? How swift is reprisal? Every day that we wake up to race toward our goal of destruction, we face a stranger. With all that we build, we forsake ourselves. Burden is reproof.

The mistaken Blame that we inflict without thought upon those who are unlike us is the burden of reproof. For that which we Blame and portend, we are Blamed. The importance of Agreement is reciprocation in Paradox.

Is it unusual to awaken in the night and to listen to the distant sounds of progress? The sounds are shrill and hurtful, yet our sense of sound is attuned and deadened. We pay no heed. The hum of electricity and the wails of sirens, traffic noise from access roads, is our music, no matter the annoyance. Hearing is the same as not hearing in life inside The R.I.P.

The Voice of It robs us of our dreams. Our destiny in sound is the scream. We listen and comply. Sound prepares us and fits us to comply. The tyranny of sound, through fear of fear, hastens our Agreement, and the mind echoes fear.

In progress, aplomb is not wanted. Progress is meant to unbalance. Equilibrium is deliberately cut off at the ears. Given enough noise, the feeling mind strays from regard: Progress requires disregard.

When one thinks in terms of art, what is it that we must choose? If one selects to live for art, does he deny life or does he create life? An artist who will not sell himself is aloof. Solitude is not binding.

There are human beings who live the equal of a thousand years within the stretch of only a choice few. Others live in Half Life and do not live at all, no matter that they reach the age of ninety. Every breath that they take is by rote and Reason and belief and training. For those in Half Life, creation is a dead chamber. In Half Life, art has no meaning beyond ticket and price, contrivance and consumption. To render art with a mind in R.I.P. is the same as living life without breath. What are brush strokes without feeling? What are words that cannot be stripped away to expose?

When one can be accused of zealotry in solitude, one has reached the pinnacle of his art in creation, because to be so accused, one must have crossed over into boundaries that have been unknown or limited in Paradox. To reach resolve in mind, one attains grace in disposition and temperament. To the being in resolve beyond R.I.P., jealousy and anger can have no meaning, for one's specific purpose and singularity are braced, not in group-think, but in Self. Individuality seeks no acclimation or proof. If solitary distinction is zealotry, it is zealotry by group proclamation. Therefore, the zealot has a dignity that those who embrace the adaptation of Reason cannot possess. The Reason of others cannot affect him. If his goal is to accomplish, then he will accomplish because he has no other purpose. His critics will fall.

The individual in Self-resolve welcomes criticism, because critical thought, through Self-doubt and Self-approbation, fuels the fire of creation and separates one further from the truth of group thought. Groups based on joint Agreement are far more dangerous than an individual who lives separately and is branded a zealot.

The zealot is detached and indifferent, yet his life, in introspection and creation, is rich and full through Resolution of will. The life in will is multitudinous and dimensional. One who may be pegged as zealot can never accept the mono-dimensional definition of green tree.

The zealot, in critical thought, cannot accept Provoker Function as exploitive method. The zealot sees until he sees, hears until he hears, and lives until he dies. His life is composed of the senses: the generation of the five that integrate to six.

To the individual thinker, called zealot by those in Agreement to fail, graciousness is his fealty to refusal.

The individual thinker, called zealot, has no Reason to fail. Fear, through doubt, is his companion. Trust is misdeed; and love, by trust, is disease by convention and contract for trade. Misery is always a promise away.

Nothing is important except that which is made, and that which is made is made in imagination of the altered state.

NOTES

NAME: DATE:

XVII

——— XVII ———

THE MEMBERSHIP

Pack Brain Mentality

"It's a poor sort of memory
that only works backwards,"
the Queen remarked.

—Lewis Carroll
Through the Looking Glass

THOSE IN OPPOSITION SAY, "WORDS MEAN SOMETHING!"

Words mean nothing. Words are props and tackles that are rigged in imagination. Words are useful in altered state only. They are sub-parallel grandiosity and theater. Words work only as much as they work us. Words provoke us and move us as we have been taught that they will provoke us and use us. Word use invalidates Self and allocates even the most simple acts of volition sparingly. The word is comptroller of our every deed. We listen to the voice of the word and we absorb it visually. We heed the word, and we use it as a mask over feeling. We marry in word and we bear children in word. We love in word and we hate in word.

What is this mask called the word? What stranger lurks behind it? What is it that we shield? Is there something that is so meek and passive that we must forever lock it up; hammer it shut inside cubicles that are too closed for air? What slender thing lies behind the message? What frailty is harbored behind the deed?

If there was a place that was life beyond the word, would we go there? If we could strip away our bondage in the word, could we then be willing to notice the thing that lies behind?

Without the legacy of the word, there could be no law, and without the legacy of the word, there could be no crime. Without the law of the word, there could be nothing to disobey. With nothing to disobey, there could be nothing over which to wage war. No murder could ever be justified. Stripped of word and Reason pretense, every act of violence would be an anomaly. Seen clearly as an act foreign to The Creature that is human, through adjustment, violence would not be tolerated. The termination of the word means the undoing of rancor and all that it entails—even profit.

Symbolic parallel imposes fear through word implants. Fear is a salable commodity, the same as misery, and both are bought and sold through the business of fear—as the politics of fear and the church of fear.

Commerce and the business of trade are merely ways of doing things. Commerce is our system of barter. However, religion and politics are also businesses, and their main business is the pretense of not being a business. This pretense is, of course, hypocrisy, and hypocrisy is advertised and sold as truth.

Politics and religion are the largest manufacturers of fear in the world, and they feed from fear. Both entities harbor fear and channel it down select paths of love and hate, greed and lust, hope and absolution of righteousness. For what do we fight wars, and who favors conflict? Who imposes conflict? It is imposed by politics and religion in the fair name of virtue.

How could the color of one's skin matter to The Creature that is human except as politicized and grounded in religion, the faith of the good? Can white hate black and black hate white while brown hates white and hates black who hates brown except through belief in fantastic—except through the imposition of memory aggrandizement, through the politics of fear and the church of fear? Separation is beneficial and desirable. Who gains?

Does The Creature that is human, abject follower and earth scratcher, gain through his symbolic association with synthetic fear that it finally becomes fear of Self? For how long are we condemned to kill ourselves for benefit of false hero and God, when hero and God are no more than costly fragments of our altered state imagination? Can we afford to continue belief in the magnificence of a God and hero so mighty that they can replace the entirety of the human race? Have not already enough sons and daughters gone to the slaughter of battle for the sake of race and creed and value that are voiced and conscripted forms of Blame, within the weariness of Blame?

What wickedness is sorrow? What are the properties of a hurtful conscience? To know pain, one must have inflicted it. If we are not innocent, then what is the precise manner of our guilt? To whom and for what do we atone? Are we so arrogant to think that there could be a God who could ever accept the warranty of our guilt? Could there be a God who could authorize our guilt? What is our technique for the absolution of our sin? Does absolution come with a guarantee? If we maim and kill for a cause, and if we atone for certified fear, should there not be a guarantee? We would demand such a thing from business. The hypocrisy of the politics and church of fear, brandished as truth, leave them exempt from the furnishing of a guarantee. Proof is in policy, yet God and hero have no policy, and yet we believe.

The precise manner of human guilt is neglect, and we have no guilt in the manner of our neglect. Retrograde Man is unworthy of guilt: If he could reach guilt, he could turn from disregard to regard. Face to face with the manner of his guilt, The Creature below Retrograde could understand the manner of his joy, for joy is the manner of release.

There can be no Reason voiced that is not Reason heard. We hear and we obey. Subjects of hero and God are the servants to the Voice of It.

Who can dare to cross that line? Philosophy crawled to the precipice but lacked the faith to go inside. Psychology, the pilferer, is a religion with many vendors, and its faithful are cowards in search of a way out.

Is it an act of faith that is required to cross over from bound truth in time and into the here and Now? Do we cherish our misery so well that we could choose misery over delight in our senses? Do we require the sanction of law and license for the pursuit of something that could be like happiness? Must happiness be Agreed happiness in order to be happiness?

Who dares to cross the line from drudgery? Is it possible to slither and roll one's way up to something that could be like God, come to it face to face, and then back down? Must we ever take the craven's course of capitulation?

There is refuge in words. There is refuge in failure. What Retrograde, the bondsman, calls his peace, is his cowardice. Retrograde, the bondsman, has membership in cowardice. Membership requires timidity.

Intelligence, The Creature, is the discernible reflection of Self in something that is like a tidal pool. Sensorial intelligence, without miasma, ebbs and flows. Rational sensorial intelligence has no purpose and requires no method. Intelligence is the seeing without seeing and the hearing that does not hear a voice. Sightless and mute, with senses joined, The Creature has no need of harmony, for his harmony is acceptance and awareness of his own inherent discord.

The Creature, disjoined from Reason Agreed, comes face to face with silence, and through silence, fear is touched. Face to face with fear, Reason falters. Failsafe loses time and momentum is stopped.

How do we calculate time? It is measured in pain and dread. We relish our misery and cling to it because we treasure time.

Freed from false suffering, we fear to find ourselves adrift and without time.

Time is a mirage of safety. We are dead when we are born and the myth of life is in the mind.

If time is an illusion, then slavery is an illusion.

If slavery is an illusion, must we yet obey?

If imagination is ruler of the altered state, then what could be imagination if we refused to imagine alteration? What if we imagined the splendor of Self? What if we imagined celebration of The Creature and acted upon it in mute solidarity?

Beyond Reason, hope is not necessary. Face to face with The Creature, can we afford to remain the faithful? Disparity is honor—bestowed, vainglorious and due.

Rapture is the release from atonement and servitude and the release from counterfeit misery. Joy through Self is knowledge that cannot be sold. No physician can prescribe it and no legislator can enact it. Celebration requires no enrollment. Agreement destroys it.

The voice of made fear is the voice of a mind and body at Impasse. Contingency is based on blind fear. We conform to Reason based on fear because we do not know it and will not know it. Pacification of life is our creed. Our code is the will to ignorance. Our method is the legacy of horror. Slavery, through ignorance, is taught.

Impassionment is the passing, through fear, to the place where the senses can be freed. Place is beyond the grasp of Reason Intent. It is the combination of the working senses, through Self-interrogation, to the workable condition of one. It is the permanent place of will. It is the touching of The Creature that is human, who still lives, who even in his natural awkwardness is perfect—who is moving to annihilate himself for Reason on the banks of future past in the name of Entity, for time.

The living Creature cannot be struck down by law, and religion, beside it, is paltry, exposed as folly in costume and the God of masquerade; the God of fashion and style.

Reason is the will to obliteration. Impassionment is the will to man. Through doubt, everything can be revealed. We are all party to a hoax. Exposed in the bright light of the living human Creature, nothing is real and everything expands. There is no duty to unsolicited truth; no boundaries and borders. Freed to illusion, all things are possible. In illusion, there can be no dread.

Without the control of Fear, The Creature unfurls. The more that we relinquish in the name of Reason, the more that we become something other than human.

Membership is the dullness of conformity in Half Life.

Membership does not include The Creature called human. We are no longer governed by our genetic codes. We are governed by the codes of science that are assigned.

NOTES

NAME: DATE:

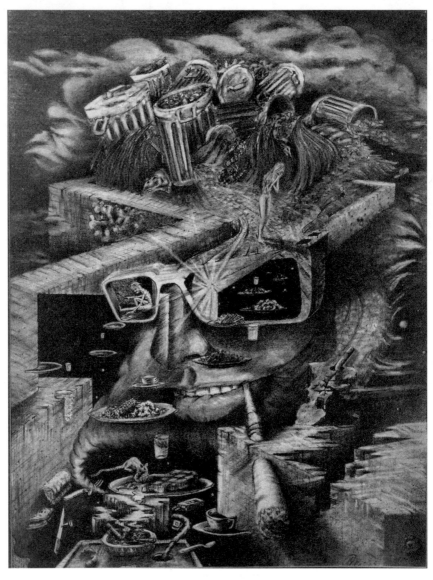

XVIII

—————— XVIII ——————

THE GREAT DECEIT

Inversion Perfected: The Agreement Process

> The doctrine that the cure for the evils
> of democracy is more democracy is like
> saying that the cure of crime is more crime.
>
> —Menchen

DECEIT, ACCORDING TO COMMON DEFINITION, is the act of being lied to or cheated. Deceit is fraud, and it is the kind of final misrepresentation that can delude or trick.

Since this is such a clear definition in lexicon, we must attempt to understand it as it is written and to come to terms with it. What is the largest deceit ever perpetrated?

Most people prefer to pretend that the great deceit does not exist. The more convoluted and massive that the deceit becomes, the more determined and fixed becomes the pretense. The pretense that the great deceit does not exist becomes part of the deceit. How easy it is to relinquish one's responsibility by declaring, "Well, that is just the way it is and has been always and will be always."

This is our convenient ready-made fix. This is societal disregard. This is the moral answer. This is ignorance and constriction—the very root that is the pillaging of the human essence. Our contentment is our destruction. We expect to be cured of our ills when the illness is us. We are the pollution, and we are the plague. We look for The Great Deceiver to set the standards of our Blame, when The Great Deceiver is us, made by They Agreement.

What devil that could be in this world is our own invention. Are we yet so craven that we must perpetuate the invention of symbolic evil as denoted bad?

Can it be so difficult to take a long hard look at the parallels of our reasonable reflections? Can we not look upon our own contortions? What is the precision of our made weakness? What binds us? Is morality weakness? We will morally destroy ourselves.

We condone murder that is sanctioned and punish those who murder outside the law. The notion of evil is our hypocrisy. We shrink from cannibalism, yet in the reasonable and lawful name of war, we consume and are consumed. What is most evil that is not a timed reflection of ourselves? In disregard, we think ourselves better.

What is the strength of our morals? Morality is the shoring up of Agreed and acceptable facade. What we call our moral fortitude is paper thin. We have no morals. We have lassitude and defect.

We vote morality and we pray morality. In sorrow, we vote and pray to a false god for false value.

Who is the keeper of our sins? Do we give over our sins to some made god, or do we mentally hang ourselves by one thin thread and dangle somewhere between technology and ritual? "To be or not to be" is the final moral question. Beyond that, there is only valor. Pity is the watchman inside the burning tower. The human beast is an inferno. With what rectitude and austerity do we mask our fear? When the walls of Reason collapse, how long can we survive in The R.I.P.?

Throughout millennia, contention does not change—only the method of its facade.

Part of the great deceit is the changing of facades. We are content, in our safety, that nothing ever changes. Yet, we deplete our resources in the name of progress and convince ourselves that time is progress, and place all value on time as though we believe that time is standing still. Time, in the form of ersatz momentum, is moving at such a fantastic rate of speed that the human being individually cannot comprehend it. Time is moving so fast that we are consuming ourselves now faster even than we can produce ourselves. Production is consumption. We can no longer deceive fast enough to assume increasing jobs that are not productive but that are consumptive.

Eventually, the human Creature, as a race and a specie, will meet itself in full circle, face to face. There will come a time of reckoning, and payment will be due. Is there a way to replace all that has been bilked in the name of progress? Can scars and craters be filled? Can prisoners of political wars be returned?

Is there a way to place the human heart back within its cavity in the chest, or has Reason seized its place so well that the heart of the human being has been transposed—completely inverted? Can there live a Creature who has no heart but who can call himself human, or has the entity of We finally progressed so thoroughly that the human being has become something else?

What falseness and what great deceit has become our hoax? What is the nature of our hollowness? What shall be the replacement of the human race?

The great deceit is our continued belief in a reality that is no more than a set of constraints and arbitrary holds that preclude the human Creature. What we contend and boast as reality is tempered idolatry of sanctified Reason and present disregard. If we can imagine misery and bear misery and willfully succumb to misery, how can it be so difficult to imagine splendor that is not inductive—that is the silence of the human flesh, mind and body in resolve? Who sets the parameters of imagination?

Future and past do not exist. They are the artifacts of implanted memory. We are taught carefully to memorize. Measurements of intelligence are based on ability to memorize, and we are rewarded based on our quantity of memory.

Remembrance is our basis for the fakery of change. All that can be stored in memory is symbols, and in symbols there is no virtue but glory.

Truth does not matter. Symbolic truth is monolithic. Symbolic truth, as myth, is transcendent of truth. There is no greater truth than the lie. Desperation, in R.I.P., is our only truth.

Artistry is not based on memory, and beyond mere cleverness, it is not prized. Art, as a probe, is dangerous to entity, for it penetrates and prods and questions Impasse memory. Reason, as propensity to recall, does not warrant question. Reason, as Paradoxical memory, disposes of it. Interrogation has no place in past or future. Zero space, place of the last parallel of man, animadversion concluded, is doubt resolved.

Memory is as far from the original intelligence of man as The Retrograde is from the heart of man. The great deceit denotes memory as the measurement of intelligence and rewards it through prizes that are memory enhanced; and memory reciprocated. Memory signifies acceptable motion and the scornful pride of Retrograde Man in disregard: The human being is distanced from life by memory.

Reason must have the reciprocation of itself to understand its own Reasons. Feeling sees into itself without the reflection of parallels. The wholeness of Sixth Sense deductive capacity is called intelligence. From portent to Intent, Reciprocation In Paradox, R.I.P., consumes The Creature called Intelligence. Nature has no recall: Without memory, there can be no Intent.

Memory is the crux of R.I.P. in consciousness. Without memory, there could be no past and future of misery to sell. This is how memory is measured as timed intelligence and valued. Time is for sale, and memory, masked as intelligence, is both its proponent and virtual slave. There is every accrual in strategic time, but there is no autonomy. Every gain in time is time distorted and the human being reduced.

Every gain in time is intelligence ventured. Time sets the distorted odds. In made time, humanity will always lose, and this is the great deceit. We trade intelligence for the values of loss and gain. By so doing, we trade intelligence for sorrow. Sorrow is wrought by made time, and it is marked against the fullness of our hearts. Situational sorrow, as forebear of Reason, kills and must kill.

Within the remnants of our humanity, there are no gauges. Machines run on instrumentation and locks. There is no kindness in speed. Machines make no apologies for the consumption of human flesh. Machines run on memory. The human being, becoming Retrograde in enterprise of Reason and in memory exchange, bears mechanical intelligence. Intelligence that is provoked by memory is speed.

Processed speed, in entity, is the master of time-voice. Speed is the master of sorrow.

If there is trickery from the master of sorrow, then whom do we pity? Can we find pity, inside the timed mechanisms of our hearts, for those who rob us of the proprietorship of Self? Can pity for our eradicators be worth the sorrow of an enslaved heart?

If the mechanics of pity have the same worth as the sorrow of human intelligence, then what worth is Self? Self, according to time, is worthless. Self, according to time, is vanity, and vanity is without pity. If one has no pity, then one is worthless to entity, for the cleverness of pity is its justification of an end.

Pity has a domino effect. In economic terms, pity may be called repeal. Politically, it may be called consensus, and in religion, it may be falsely called zeal.

The heart of pity is a heart of destruction. What Retrograde pities most he destroys most. Wars are started on the premise of pity and an artificial heart of goodness. Reasoned pity has a counterfeit heart.

A heart of darkness is a Reasoned heart, and the heart in Reason will not wait. It moves on. If pity could be something like compassion, the heart of Self could be slowed, and slowed, the Self can become aware of life.

Many human beings, in the middle of their lives, rebuke system's speed and overload. Many give up, and in private sadness, below The R.I.P., wait for an obscure end to what they know is not life. They wait for the end of waste while wasting away.

Others spend the bulk of their lives looking for magic—the formula or the key or the potion that they can drink freely and gain from it profound and secret wisdom. They forfeit.

What could be one long and gracious day, blended in subtle rotations of day and night, is shattered into myriad cutting shards that are the dismal days and nights of Paradox. Paradise is split. We live inside The R.I.P. We live inside the dungeons of our own reflections: our expectations and sorrows. Duty served is duty earned. There is no recompense for life.

Duty affectation is founded in Blame. Retrograde, the future machine, fears Blame and gives allegiance to Blame as it comes full circle. Retrograde safeguards justified future and holds to residual history no matter how grim are his tales of false victory and bondage. Retrograde, the human inverse, with the blood of his circumstantial martyrs and saints on his hands, is not worthy even of guilt.

Guilt does not Blame. Human culpability, without Intent, felt through to the thin marrow of The Creature, questions the comfort of vainglorious Self-disdain and gives to intelligence the full responsibility of change.

Guilt by belief is not atonement. Atonement is retribution for dutied sin, and sin is the religion of invented right.

To feel full guilt is to know fallacy as warrant and justification. The understanding of the synthetic guilt of The Retrograde is the beginning of Self-awareness. In Paradox, everyone pays a penalty. Life is a business, and no one is exempt from authorized impunity. Guilt realized is the separation from guilt. Those who can recognize guilt through participation drop out. They can have no need of camaraderie: Guilt is guilt by association.

Safety in numbers is part of the great deceit. There is no safety.

Truth, en masse, is harm. The individual thinker is harmed. The group is conditionally failsafed, and it is exempt from the harm of its truth because truth, en masse, is group manufactured and group obeyed.

When one steps away from Agreement, one is no longer bound by strategic truth. No longer bound, one is at liberty to imagine other than altered-state reality.

When one can manipulate and control illusion, one is privy to the entrusted lie—that the ultimate deceit is the ultimate freedom. Freedom accrues commerce and commerce sells freedom: Money is privilege.

To imagine beyond Reason is intuition beyond the mental fields of either made truth or circumstantial lie. Imagination beyond justification is imagination that requires neither commercial freedom nor constriction because imagination beyond the rigid pretense of altered state is the sublime imagination of original joy.

When will we find capacity to imagine the fair images of the human heart—the vastness that lies beyond our constrictions of fact and fable?

To deceive a deceiver is not deceit. Thus, we live in deception pro rata.

NOTES

NAME: DATE:

NOTES

NAME: DATE:

XIX

XIX

KNOWLEDGE THAT IS *NOT*

Ersatz Momentum Settled

As soon as questions of will or decision
or reason or choice of action arise,
human science is at a loss.

—Professor Noam Chomsky

THERE IS A PRECOCIOUS ELEMENT TO THIS TITLE; and this is intentional. The Reason for its loftiness is for the stark verification of the precocity of knowledge; its amplitude and breadth; its absolute correctness.

The parallel of feeling to Reason directs question to the center of introspective, critical thought. Feeling to Reason is the excavation of knowledge implication for use as an internal tool. Feeling to Reason produces the tingling beneath the skin that incites organic understanding—the removal of layer after layer of nomenclature until the substance of critical thought can be seen and tasted.

Knowledge is a societal tool intended to teach and to promote its teachings through justification of belief. The teaching of knowledge carries false hope of wisdom. Wisdom wrought from knowledge plants made truths in the minds of human beings from which it is expected that more truth will grow. When such truth, as belief, falters, it is modified or altered so that it can blend into the rest of held knowledge—the factors of Belief that are taken from other summarily grounded abridgments.

When a child refuses to learn in the assigned manners and coded expectations of written and verbal knowledge, he is

penalized first and ostracized second, and made to believe that
he is less, third. To become a part of acceptable entity, it is
mandatory to master the censored Second Voice. If the child
continues to rebuke proscribed knowledge, his mind will be
educationally truncated to fit into the necessary parameters of
it. He will be assigned a diagnosis. He will be cut off from mainstream knowledge and given over to other venues of that which
are considered educational paths of specialty. He will be said to
have a knowledge disability, and his consumption of knowledge
will then be relegated and consigned to the penalty of special
dominion. More words and more symbols, along with drug use,
will be prescribed for the malady that does not exist except as
made to exist for profit.

In knowledge selling, the intelligence of The Creature does
not matter, because what is bought and sold is not intelligence,
but is conformity and subjugation to knowledge as written and
as taught. The more that a child is willing to conform to restrictions, the more that he is praised and rewarded as supremely
gifted and supremely intelligent. Those who resist this bondage
are bound tighter to it by the fact of their resistance, as diagnosed by medicine and law. Those who are not willing to sell
themselves are, through the rightful belief factor of knowledge,
sold over into it by those in possession of certification to do so.

A child is a child because he is not indoctrinated. A child is a
child as long as he is free and his opinions are unrestrained
and unabashed. When a child begins to lose his natural lack of
inhibition, he is becoming not a child; is losing First Voice in
original Self. Knowledge, indoctrinated, reduces the human
being so that he is fit to enter the fold.

In this way, large resources of intelligence are wasted. How
can we know what can be accomplished when we rush to squash
it before it can bloom?

When a child refuses the teachings of Paradox, he is sharply
rebuked by entity and its rewards. Such a child, in his inherently human First Voice, has lesser value in entity, and his lack-

ing, which is fullness, is judged disability. Disabled, disagreement is contained.

Since Agreement is enabled, we push our children to excel within its set borders of mediocrity and indifference. This is the value of knowledge, and its final value is indemnified disregard. The smart become the feeble, and they are paid well for their feebleness. The feeble are valued for their memory only.

Intelligence has no reward. Intelligence must make its own way. An intelligent man may prosper, but it will be by his own devise and not by the dangling want of the prize in future past.

Civilized man, The Retrograde, is the slave of knowledge. No one is exempt. Even one who sets himself apart from the Agreement Process does so after the fact of his initial Agreement. There is little choice in this because we are bound over to knowledge as children before we have experience to discern and before we have backing, or the conviction of mind, to stand alone—before we have Resolution to disagree. A child has little chance against grown-up chattel. We force our children into Agreement because we have agreed. There is no other way, because any other way has already been marketed and sold by Agreement. We force our children to fail because we have failed.

Knowledge enabled is an artifact of sorrow—a template for bondage—and it is method by exclusion.

Knowledge is symbolic voice. Through our mental, emotional gates, we realize much more what is not than what is made to exist, and we realize that what is said to be knowledge is questionable. Through Self-interrogation, we find that when we lead, we follow, and when we think, we amend.

When we teach, we placate, and when we medicate, we anesthetize. Reciprocals of processed thought are implanted in the civil mind and make for a covering film of fancy and fraud that conceals the Self from Self. The Self is not a Creature of truth but a thing of feeling, and feeling is not solid but liquid and vapor.

The Self dissolves into feeling and blends. The joy of Self is the release from made truth. Release from made truth is the release from bondage in entity. How could it feel to know pleasure that cannot stop; that is not based on false premise nor on arbitrated promise; not on temporal Agreement? How must it feel to live without Reason—with the dignity of Self-composed Self? What could be the bounty of the human mind if knowledge had no value; no price?

If knowledge was not a commodity, the human mind would have no limit in its reach and capacity. With knowledge devalued, knowledge could be knowledge that is instead of that which is not, and knowledge that is not would no longer be warranted and credited.

Knowledge that is not is the destruction of the human being at the beginning of its assent to learn. It is the thwarting of the desire to understand and create. We use it to destroy in the name of progress, and we use it to destroy in the name of interest and in the name of appeasement. Education is not an instrument of learning. It is an institution for control. It is an institution for the sale and distribution of knowledge and for the penalizing of those who cannot constitutionally adhere to its narrow methods of detainment.

The unabridged Reason of the human being, through feeling, is critical, deductive thought. Deduction is the taking away of Reason all the way down to feeling until Reason is resolved. Through deduction, we can know what is by what is not, and we know, not because we have been taught to know, but because we have doubted—down to the place where the mind, in the splendor of its senses, can find freedom that has no price.

Knowledge that is not is knowledge by omission. The living Creature is omitted—the frail thing that longs to see and hear and touch and taste and smell—without penalty and without price. Self is omitted in favor of time because time is the payment of knowledge.

In time we are paid to abandon ourselves; paid to tear our substance of being in two; paid well for the mental trespass enacted by knowledge through Reason. With knowledge, we are paid to abandon our children or to pay them off in time for progress.

We omit with intention, and our intention is justified and guaranteed. We are guaranteed safety in Half Life. But is safety worth our bargaining of Self? Is knowledgeable omission worth the selling of our only life?

When we sell ourselves into knowledge and into knowledge belief through certification, we are cordoned from ever knowing the thing that is without fear. We are sold the idea that one's symbolic good is of greater value than the completeness of Self; that the educated Second Voice is more capable, while the intrinsic First Voice has no capacity at all.

Belief is the sealing of made and justified fear, and knowledge is concordant with belief. We are restricted and constrained in knowledge belief. The interrogation of factors of belief offers no surety. Question exacts a heavy toll: Omission is by Agreement.

All that is not sensorial is imagined, and in the life of the sense, real does not matter. Imagine a world where made-to-mean reality is not a base and you will imagine a world without pain! A world without pain is a world without hope and without pity. That which was always real was real before the human being ever touched it. Knowledge is reality based in inversion, and reality is functional adhesion that is imagined—symbolically skewed and manipulated.

We have rigged together a synthetic world that exists side by side with a sensual world that has no pretense to reality as shared belief. Sensuality is timeless, has no value in memory, and cannot be bought or sold. Reality, as functional adhesion to bought knowledge, is sub-parallel belief that is false. The sensual world is not false because it does not subjugate. The world of the senses is subjective and cannot penalize.

The sensing that the human being has for a bodily home is his quest for aloofness from the constraints of reality made by others. In the sensual home, The Creature exerts itself, explores endlessly, and finds place that is not necessarily a constructed abode but is a mental place where the mind can free itself to stretch and relax. Home, to the thinking Creature, is place that is without price. Home to The Creature is freedom to search and delineate without restriction; to adjust all need and want.

Ideal residences are ones that are remote—in deep forest lands or on mountaintops or close to the ocean. Sold into entity and in Agreement with it, many people then seek seclusion from it. We earn seclusion from it even as we barter for it and defend it and rationalize it. Residential seclusion is like a badge of honor for having succumbed.

How can we Agree so adamantly with what we so plainly, loathe? Do we so pity The Retrograde that we take refuge even from ourselves? What is home but a primal desire for original Self? The sense for home is a sense for nature; original place; the child that is sensitive and open; place where not one Reason ranks higher than Self-awareness.

Knowledge that is not capable of the inclusion of feeling is devoid of human purpose. Knowledge that is not is not human purpose but intention in entity. Knowledge, as it is used in entity, is duty because those who invest in it and subscribe to it are duty-bound to demonstrate it. Those who are rewarded for duty must endure the drudgery of it. Condemnation to mediocrity exacts a heavy toll. Those who endure for the rewards of duty are themselves dispatched to glorify it—gilt misery made an artifact of time.

No matter the physical comforts of their homes or luxuries afforded, such duty-bound creatures sense that something is missing from their lives. In the sense that something is missing, they sense The R.I.P. and the split of the parallels of Reason and feeling.

Emotional feeling is *a priori* First Voice. We are born fully functional in feeling and naked of Reason, fully aware of our environment and needs. Helpless to meet our own needs, we are sensitive to changes in our environment and we respond to changes through our senses. When we are cold, we scream.

When we need food, we scream and food is given. The scream is without implanted Reason because it is of original importance. If left unhindered and intact, the scream becomes resolution to comprehend. The human being has a natural inclination to explore and to know. Left alone by the cropping of knowledge—the shortening of duty to knowledge, the schemes and Reason making of knowledge—the original human mind has thirst to decode and to undo—to discover beyond all knowledge and institution. Stunted early in life, we settle for payment of duty and knowledge that has been bought and maintained. We settle for Half Life. We know nothing but The Word.

Knowledge that is not is made-meant-to-mean the intention of the group. Group concern is symbols upgrade for status and power. Symbols upgrade raises the price of knowledge. In symbols upgrade, the characters of right and good are enlarged until knowledge that is not becomes the order and protocol of the workplace. Knowledge that is not sanctions noun inversion and fantastic Reason. Mandatory meetings are held for purpose that is not and productivity is non-productivity. Those who have purpose that is are considered mavericks and to be lacking in team spirit or management ability. The human qualities of these people are considered flaws by those duty-bound to knowledge that is not. Energy is directed at cost-cutting that does not cut costs but does cut service and quality. Speed demands the thinking of a machine without interruption or complaint. The human being is slow and doubtful and he is pushed to the extreme.

Dedication is made to the re-engineering of the work force when nothing is re-engineered except in word, and jobs are lost, and those charged to re-engineer are given to create task that is not. Task that is not outlines its movements in careful diagrams to show what it is not doing that is being done for progress that is not.

The realm that is not is the realm of The Retrograde, diametrical man in antithetical nature—the human inverse. In the split world of The R.I.P., sense is nonsense and nonsense is sense. Future is obsolete. Reason, in entity, has run its course. We are consuming ourselves. The will to omission is the will to the cannibal.

Silence in the face of annihilation is commitment by unraised question. We are all accomplices. There is no excuse.

Sold into knowledge and cast into the labyrinth of lexicon, we see that Reason reciprocals go awry before the font of the non-symbolic human mind, stunningly adrift in a vital and opulent sea. To relinquish Reason means a release into eternal space that is the womb of eternal life.

NOTES

| NAME: | DATE: |

XX

THE CREDIT/DISCREDIT GAME

Believable Delusion and Grandeur

Man is only a reed,
the weakest thing in nature;
but he is a thinking reed.

—Blaise Pascal

To GAIN CREDIT, one agrees with whatever frame of current mental standing has mass appeal. One is willing to change his thoughts quickly as dictated by caprice. One agrees to sell himself for Agreement to obtain functional license and certified purpose that may have no purpose. This is subscription to knowledge as it is being used. This is knowledge for sale.

One who disagrees is discredited by group sanction. Those who are discredited and who will not agree will not be believed. One who cannot be believed defies belief. One who, through his willing disagreement and through his selective search for purpose, creates. One who disagrees and, by his own capacity and resolve to create, surpasses Agreement and uses knowledge without rightful purchase and without paid subscription is the man who has no fear and who is feared.

One who creates himself outside Agreement creates from the fine dust and ashes of agreed fear and composes agreed dread. The creator of Self has witnessed the possibility of annihilation through group loyalty. The sentient Self-creator is one who has defied belief and defied made fear to step through the mirrored images of all that is made-meant-to-mean by the inversions of Paradox. The sentient Self-creator is one who has stepped through the looking glass of Reason and into the antithesis of Reason. Symbolically, the Self creator is one who has journeyed to hell and back.

All thought is corollary. Deduction of paralleled match in Reason is feeling. Feeling that has no match is resolve. There is no transition through emotion that can be given a name. Named, emotion becomes fixed and contrite in its station. Named, it is not emotion.

The noun called love is apologetic and recreant and is based on Reason. Love exacts promise and becomes love for Reason. Deduced, the emotion that we name love is liquid and clear. The emotion that we name love cannot be stunted by promise nor by the seeming breakage of promise. Love that is emotion with no parallel match has no end. Love that is credited in bondage is exacting and scrupulous. Those who refuse to promise intention are without credit and are without love and without virtue.

One is discredited when one has not been paid. To receive credited certification, one need not be so much clever as willing and able to make payments in order to receive payments. Not only must one be willing and able to make payments to the god of currency, one must also be willing to make incremental payments of will to earn place in Paradox—to earn place to manipulate. Method replaces volition. In order to achieve credit in Paradox, the human being sells his essence. Success is willful decline. In latter-day R.I.P., those who succeed are those who obey. We do so for Blame and for wretchedness within the circle of Blame. Condemnation is the circle of sadness in which we dwell. Misery sells.

Those who are less certified pay those who are more certified. However, in Paradox, Blame Loop is complete when those who are most blamable are granted, by lawful aggregation, full power to Blame. Those who have paid, both in money and in the relinquishing of increments of will over time, become by writ even more blamable than the original blamed. Those empowered are at the mercy of those who have no power except the power of conscription. Knowledge certification ultimately brings less authority to Blame than the massive will to ignorance. Those who have paid dearly for knowledge certification are subject to the whim and caprice of ignorance. Those who set forth to collect upon the vagrancy of ignorance are made accountable to ignorance. Reason for Reason becomes fantastic and Blame is passed circuitously, as in a loop, from the credited blamers to the discredited blamed, back and forth, again and again, until ersatz momentum—time motion—is made Agreed Progression.

All suffering is false because all remedy is false. All suffering is false because it is manufactured and sold as Reason. The treachery of anguish and the deceit of misery are legacy. Original sorrow is original man extinguished. As we approach obsolescence, it is our failure to Self-resolve that designates the human being to antiquity. Giving over to will mechanization and will that is ironclad enactment, the human Creature contracts.

We will be replaced by our own contrivance: Retrograde, the human inverse. What we affirm as life is ruse. Half Life is stratagem. In Half Life, suffering is guaranty. In life that has no strategy, there is no guaranty. All suffering is false and placation is counterfeit. Outside time and outside Agreement, there is no legacy of grief. The cycle of Blame is the cycle of disregard and the heritage of scorn. With malicious caprice, we place one another in shame: Credit and discredit, through Blame and abomination, deliver us worthy of shame. The false notions of good and evil supplant emotion until what could be emotion becomes false deed and mental undoing. Suffering is always for Reason and shame is its made duty.

The certified serve the forbidden and the forbidden govern. In Blame Loop, knowledge is contraband until purchased. Knowledge held for Reason and made liable cyclically to castigation by commission has no conclusion beyond reasonable proof. Material is made failsafed product of construed malevolence, and its proof is reproof. Within a cycle of Blame, knowledge is the legacy of grief. What does knowledge signify except Self-uselessness? What, besides knowledge technology, has changed in two thousand years? Has knowledge expunged conflict and starvation?

As long as knowledge is held within the continuum of condemnation, it has no purpose beyond purposelessness and the imitation of progress. Knowledge as value is knowledge that denotes Blame and delivers Blame. One who, by rote intelligence that is feebleness, believes that knowledge is providence, is a believer in dogma that is the blind will to ignorance. Statute in squalor is law in reprimand. There is no proof but Blame. Justice served is The Creature decried. We are severed from paradise by knowledge implant and The R.I.P. is complete.

The R.I.P. of knowledge is the privilege of use that, in context of cyclic condemnation, is neglect: the present disregard. Noun stacking is implanted by rote. The privilege of neglect is connoted and inferred by method of noun usage. Privilege is not earned: It is bought, and it is bought by Agreement to function. One cannot acquire privilege unless one agrees to agree.

Entitlement is endowment of creed. Entitlements convey belief. In Paradox, entitlement is proof of worth. The veracity of noun privilege is not questioned. Love is connoted good and hate is connoted evil without question, when mirrored through the mind, all nouns are altered state inversions. That which we love we also, by the inversion of the mind, hate, and that which we hate is given honor, for we are taught to possess what we love. Once we possess, the emotion that is called love is violated.

How else could the world, in Reasonable R.I.P., have become such a plethora of spasmodic hopes and joys made lame by the burlesque of Reason? Noun privilege is travesty. Noun privilege is affirmed neglect.

Retrograde Man, ever fearful of the Beast who still lives inside, becomes what he fears the most. Too frightened to step through inversions of Self, his gentle inquisitor, he falls upon the deposing rank of privilege as redeemer. Through bought redemption, he acquires knowledge as material and becomes, himself, a commodity of Reason. Bought and sold into the privilege of neglect, the human inverse, Retrograde, is sanctioned by law and fanciful conciliation to plunder for the name of Reason. Hypocrisy is perfected. Progress is annihilation. Refusal to recognize the human Beast is to become a thing in a prison: How easy it is to contort the Beast of compassion into a mind of hate. We do so for Reason and we do so for dread. We do so for noun privilege and for credit: We are what we most fear.

All that does not move can be crushed. The penalty for disagreement is banishment. When one steps outside the facade of time, one can expect to live alone, but no longer as a willing victim. When one, through doubt, rebukes empowerment and resist the privilege of neglect—shirks the legacy of grief—he can expect to have no friend in Reason. Trust and faith; love and hope; knowledge and progress—all fall apart before the oracle of fear.

Fear offers no promise—no gain. Fear is the repentance of nothing: the atonement of nothing. The resolve to zero is undaunted by Reason and unhastened by progress. Resolve is immovable and yet cannot be crushed. Resolve that is the human will uncompromised dissolves all hindrance. Blame is the enemy of no Blame. The human will uncompromised has no impediment. The will to stillness has no antithesis and no antecedent. Original calm is parallel to original Self.

Tangled always in artificial webs of intrigue by lethal selection and through the privilege of neglect, Intelligence, The Creature, spins fine barriers to separate him from complete sensual awareness and the riches of Self.

We affirm too quickly and we realize too late the faint borderlines of Self that we have obscured by scheme or cabal. Too late does the human being realize that he has never sensed a tree—that what he took to mean green tree was nothing other than a blank notion, flat and inconsequential. Too late, The Creature becomes fixed and immobile in resolve. Like the flesh of an oyster, the human being senses an irritation that he cannot name; feels the tug and pull that is like a current.

By the will to ignorance, he longs to name what he deems malady and to find remedy and refuge, when always the disease has been provocation to made duty, nearly from birth.

What we name disease could as well be diagnosed as denial of life and failure to live. Illness that has no foundation in bacterium and virus, nor in malignancy of cells, nor in the wearing away of organs, is not disease but catastrophic myth and degeneration through Agreement to fail. To brand as diseased is authority to administer drugs that sell another's will into slavery. We sell ourselves over to disease and scramble for cure when there is no cure for failure to live. In R.I.P., we live on placebos and time.

How silly does The Creature appear when cloaked in the paper garb of his credit like a show dog decked out and groomed for competition—the demeanor of a once graceful and amiable animal contorted and defaced for Reason!

Credit makes of us flimsy and pasty things. The more credentials that we seek and hold the more that we succumb to duty and its accouterments. The more deeply that we allow ourselves to become enslaved to duty, the more credit that we receive. The more credit that we receive, the more we are enslaved.

Blame Loop is written in duty. When we earn and gain credit, we lose. When we debase ourselves in order to earn credit or to discredit others, we lose. In Blame Loop, gain is always by contention, and gain is hollow when it is marked by the loss of humanity.

In the darkness of the night mind—or in the first moments of dawn—we can know ourselves. What is it that we know? Are we the figments of credit that are distributed as worth, or are we creators of Self that know no fear?

NOTES

NAME: DATE:

XXI

XXI

INTELLECTUAL COLLATERAL

Power and Position and Ranking Profiteers

There are two sides to every question
because when there are no longer two sides,
it ceases to be a question.

—Blaise Pascal

A SPLIT REALITY PLACES THE ORIGINAL SELF of the human being at odds with a synthetic device that is forced momentum of The Word for production of false cause and effect that, without such synthetic contrivance, would not exist and could not be produced. Progress, the idea of advancement for betterment of future, places the human being in jeopardy of annihilation through Self-consumption and expenditure.

Intellectual collateral is that which is given for holding in promise of tomorrow. Intellectual collateral is a method of securing place that is status through surety. Surety is no more than belief. Its promise is not truth but a concordat. Truth, spurious or otherwise, has little bearing upon Agreement. Results do not matter as long as Agreement is intact. The partial fact that Agreement falls short of its promise does not stop us from agreeing. We are brought up on Agreement and spoon-fed on Agreement. From the very beginning of our remembrance of time, we are taught to agree and to comply. Language enforces Agreement. The Word is law.

Intellectual collateral is our means of existing in two parallel worlds: The parallel of Reason and the parallel of feeling. Collateral in Reason is the parallel of accomplished trust in made reality. The parallel of feeling is undemanding of reality. It does not demand payment, and in its sensual flowing of vision and hearing and smell and taste and touch, it places no value and no trust.

The world of feeling has no Reason to trust and no Reason to value. Its markings on The Creature are quiescent and serene. In feeling, silence is golden. Sounds that are free of instruction and demand are translated into silence because the sound that is silence is healing and soothing to the mind.

The voice of Reason is loud and harsh. It demands and penalizes and exacts payment. It trusts and expects complete trust in return. The voice of Reason restricts us and contorts us until intelligence does not matter, nor talent nor sensitivity. According to the voice of Reason, the only thing that matters is compliance with Agreement in Reason manifest.

Want is not a matter, because Reason proscribes want. Need does not matter, because Reason does away with need and inverts it to Reason justification. Sexual need is met with the inverted confines of marriage. Basic need to discover is met through the eyes and ears of controlled media. Need to own is met through Reasonable promise for future and atonement for past.

Within the fictional reality of Reason, Now does not exist.

Within Reason one need not think, because thinking is done in pre-thought and within the machinery of pre-thought deed and think-process.

Reason is machine, and Retrograde, the man, is its drudge. We do as we think and we think as is done to us. Question is transgression.

It can be deduced that we came to this through the loss of First Voice. Before our slavery to the machinery of words, there was a time when critical thought was esteemed. There was a time when critical thought was taught in universities. There was a time when the creation of man through thought was honorable and with dignity.

In latter day R.I.P., things are different not because of the sophistication of our machines, but because of our lack of expansion in Self—our complete disregard of the human Creature. Indeed, if we used our technology for the human being instead of for the pillage of the human race and the replacement of it, First Voice could still have expression. It is not the technology that has become overbearing but Impasse Reason and its hold on the human being—our desire to expunge ourselves.

Our knowledge system is devoted to misery and the upkeep of misery. If this were not so, there would be no need of philanthropy. Philanthropic societies exist on the premise of doing good. If everything was as good as future promise that we sell to our children, there could be no need to do further good. Good would already be done.

However, since the promise of good is a hoax, organizations for the doing of good must be employed, and good is meted out in small packages. Thematic good is done more for the conveyor of good than for the recipient of it. Small increments of good do very little to ward off human misery. Hunger is not appeased with symbolic good. Poverty is not vanquished with promised good. Good does not head off disease.

The virtue of good is not profitable unless it is warranted and charged as good. So warranted, good becomes part of the misery. Charged good is the same as evil when it is rendered for Progress.

Rendered for progress, good becomes an act of imperialism. Good is jingoistic and chauvinistic because it is an enactment of entity for the procurement of group adherents or followers. A debt of gratitude is a form of bondage. The said weak upon whom good is enacted are bound to be forever grateful to good and to the source of good. Gratitude solicits idolatry and it certifies might. The meek are the hopeless. They have no hope because all hope has been bought and sold by the hopeful to sell back to the hopeless. Hope is forever the habitat of the well-to-do. Hope and good are fraught with magnificent cunning!

Those without symbolic hope are without made fear. Without

such fear, the thinking Creature must face random, circumstantial fear alone and without abridgment. The fear of the hopeless is final. The fear of the hopeless is fear without cunning and fear that is not prostrate in gratitude. The exposure and fear of the hopeless is uncertain fear without synthetic warrant or charge.

The fear of the hopeless turns the Creature upon itself until it comes face to face with its own frailty, its own calmness, and its own parallel resolution. In First Voice, the thinking human Creature finally dissolves into itself and realizes its place and realizes that place is in joy of Self that is exempt from sorrow.

Hunger has no sorrow because hunger has no pity. Hunger has no Reason. Hunger is collateral to First Voice.

Entity entices and subjects those in fear of hunger and in fear of hopelessness. Entity is exploiter of all fear. Friendless, we are bound over to Reason Paradox. But to walk in fear is to walk the paths of joy.

To overturn splendor, as we are made to Reason, is a treacherous act upon the wholeness of The Creature.

To know love in exile is to love beyond Reason. Love unrequited is love unbound, and it is never sated. Love possessed and sated is death of love. Love possessed invests and, by its investments, it is deemed worthy in entity. Love without possession has no worth and is occult. We are taught to hide our feeling as shame no matter the ultimate cost.

Love possessed is the mask that we wear. What could be something like affection is carefully hidden behind the mask of convention. Affection is carried around like secret little bundles held close against the middle. We dare not let them be discovered when there is so much of possession at stake to gain or lose. Love does not acknowledge love but assumes and buys loyalty in the forms of Agreement and time. Affection may not be much more than a furtive glance or a stolen touch that, though its fullness cannot be mistaken, is mistaken and is mistaken with great care.

The solicitations and grandiose manners of Agreement and the important appearance of Agreement are kept no matter the hypocrisy and transparency of hypocrisy. Possessed love, no matter its petty rules and fickle demands, is esteemed and credited. Love that is without possession is kept hidden from one's friends and compeers until finally the hypocrisy is all that can remain. Hypocrisy is a blunt instrument. Its injury is the inflicting of a dull psychic ache that does not leave no matter the passage of time behind the mask.

Unrequited love without possession is a cardinal and base sin that has no other absolution than hypocrisy. At all cost to self, secret sin must be kept as secret sin. Hypocrisy conquers all.

Intellectual collateral is the parallel of the unreal beside the parallel of the made real. Made real is the realm of The Retrograde, while unreal is the home of the thinking Creature. Where these lines cross is the shaft and the enactment of The R.I.P. It is in this mental passage that inversion of meaning occurs and where sensorial comparison finds antecedent. This is the demarcation that makes life a burden and makes all possible joy no other than symbolic ritual. It is at this mental juncture that the made real polices what is assessed unreal. Made real, by its artifacts of mythic truth, disposes of feeling. Made real dictates uniformity and conformity and advocates mandatory ignorance, and by inversion invents present disregard. Made real is distributed as constituted fact and all must comply or be made to comply.

When a human being does not comply to made real, he is said to be eccentric or insane or zealous. There are those who are troubled by their failure in Agreement. These are said to have gone mad, or they are diagnosed with antisocial disorders. Without the cognizance of intellectual abilities to deduct what is troubling them, such persons seek the help of medicine. Their misery is placated and charmed.

How easy it is to become a victim or to become infirm or to become a disciple of psychological vanities. Those who hallucinate or hear voices that are not real do so as a release from provocation and conscripted failsafe. Their hallucinations are a release valve from the takeover of Reason. Such a tormented being is tormented by the pitting of the made real inversion to the substantial and emotive unreal. Since they cannot live in disregard and their fear of regard is great, they succumb to malady. Their label of affliction gives them false hope. Madness is their redemption, and their psychologist becomes their god and their relief from burden. Madness and placation of madness is a huge and profitable business.

We are idiots trusting idiots to trick us into believing that we cannot be whole and perfect if we do not live inside the boundaries of consummate hypocrisy. We are made to believe that we will disappear—that we will be swallowed up—if we do not conform to what is made real. We fear our insanity, but what is our made real world if not insane? We live in a world and are contained inside a world of inversions. We are very small puppets controlled by Reason, waiting to die with coins in our pockets.

Psychotropic drugs are expensive and premium, and they do little to relieve hallucination or delusion. The willing insane are left to dangle—to fend for themselves in a world that has no understanding and no want to understand that which is not like it.

If insanity is an act of volition, then sanity is an act of volition. The will to madness is present disregard, when what is before our eyes and at our fingertips and in our nostrils cannot be denied. Insanity is the will to Retrograde. This is the split magnified and amplified to fit a mold for marketing. All hazard is profitable.

What of the human being who has no fear because he has known fear in the breach of the human parallel of consciousness? What of the human being who has no qualm in crossing barriers in want of Self-expansion; in want of transparency of feeling; in want of completeness; in want of Reason for Reason void?

What of the human being who is successful in living life in the middle, who will not succumb to Half Life, will not become either dutifully sane or insane—who elects, through doubt, the choice of his humanity that is his intelligence. The thinking Creature is one that is willing to become his own intrinsic Self, triumphant in Self-resolve—that which is his one humanity both inside The R.I.P. and below it. What of the human being who can have no master?

Human joy, unlike misery, cannot be packaged and sold. It cannot be prescribed or prepared. It must be realized that it cannot be found inside the Paradox of The R.I.P.; lexicon and the word labyrinth reduce it. Knowledge displaces it and conformity to Reason kills it. There is no god that can bestow it and no government that can enforce it by law.

What is left? Joy of the Self is settled in Self. The path to completion is the path to the eternal Self in First Voice emotion—the will to zero place. There is no such thing as destiny unless it is the destiny of Self-determination by feeling, back through cause and effect, through fear to The R.I.P. that produced the entity of the living undead.

What of The Retrograde? He is no more than a puppet, and when we can determine that his strings can no longer be pulled, he does not exist. Seemingly strong in numbers, he is flimsy when separated from the failsafe of group. Retrograde is disposable and can be disposed as soon as we release our investment in credit—in serviceable value and its circle of Blame.

Resolve is intellectual boldness: the bond of original Self in First Voice. Reason is set in dualistic choice that is not choice but compulsion. Collateral memory is set in the blood that is our sea of made strife.

We-to-they must pay tribute to those who give over their lives in order to maintain and hold Impasse, perfect Paradox, and the same perfect hypocrisy that will be the legacy of atonement and the intellectual collateral of our children to come.

N O T E S

NAME: DATE:

NOTES

NAME: DATE:

XXII

——————————— XXII ———————————

SYMBOLS UPGRADE

Jargon, Labels & Manipulation

The Nonconformist Conscience
makes cowards of us all.

—Max Beerbohm

SYMBOLS UPGRADE IS PROGRESSIVE MIRAGE in process-think and
isolation by duty. Symbols upgrade is the rate of data in
momentum: duty made sacrosanct and correct. In symbols
upgrade, current position is held in context of tense for measurement of made time. Increments of time invention are allotted for both past and future. Future past is prerequisite for
higher learning for degrees of profit and augmented certification of the memory of Retrograde in time.

Universities do not open minds to introspective study and
expansion, but are in the business of certification, and the cost of
certification is high. Only the premium select of Retrograde gain
certification, and these are premium select by their ability to pay.
To gain certification, one must be privy to certified and certifi-
able jargon. Institutions of higher learning hold authority over
the certification of jargon and certified jargon and they sell it.

The Retrograde in symbols upgrade does not change, but he
Reasons, through think process, that change has occurred, and
that his share in momentum has increased. In think-process this
is indeed partial fact, for his interest in knowledge investiture
has increased by his purchase of it. In Half Life, at the mental
juncture of The R.I.P., the speed of Reason and Reasoned jar-

gon for nomenclature is moving at a fantastic rate.

The speed of Reason is moving at the speed of consumption. Even now, through observation of Retrograde in velocity, it may be discerned through deduction of critical thought that the human being has been usurped. Collateral of substance has run its course and waned. Given over completely to job and function, the human being has disintegrated. The Creature has folded.

Disaster for the human race has been predicted for years. It could be that disaster will not come in the form of cataclysmic event. The annihilation of a specie may be silent and go unnoticed for decades. Annihilation may not be a matter of displacement but of replacement. The difference between Retrograde and human may never be recognized. The progression to Self-annihilation is enabled by complacence and by obedience to duty.

Impasse is blind end. Impasse is the last stopping point of Reason. If it can be understood that Impasse is the last Reason fixed for intent and retained for use and re-use, it can be understood that the human race has reached a point of calamitous Paradoxical Impasse.

Our resources are depleted. Ersatz momentum is running on empty. At Impasse, we have nothing left for re-use but ourselves and what we make ourselves to mean, and what we make ourselves to mean is the manner of rightful plunder.

We are consuming ourselves. We have reached a point in the business of civilization where products are no longer produced. What is produced is consumption. The only thing that is important is consumption: We are feeding on ourselves. At the mental Impasse of Reason, The Creature is commodity, is expenditure and is disposable.

Fixed in mental Impasse of Reason, all motion is false. To move forward in symbols upgrade, Retrograde trades himself, in bondage, for Reason. His bondage guarantees his fixed status in an altered state and warrants his pledge to the inversion of Agreed altered state and his perpetuation of it no matter the absurdity. Anyone who disagrees with the legacy of altered state is downplayed as negative, and negative is connoted bad.

It is never considered that what is agreed to be negative thought could be the opening of the mind into something that is beyond the Impasse of Reason. Doubt is the beginning of mental expansion over Impasse. The negative mind is open and sinuous, its circuits winding down neural paths that are unrestricted, its cerebral trails convoluted and abundant with choice, its mental constructs capable of Reason to feeling that is unimpeded will.

No wonder that Agreement condones only Agreed Positive! It is impossible to consign virtual slavery to the negative man. Question is mental autonomy. Doubt is the path to the will of man.

Negativity is not nonconformity. The nonconformist seeks alternative methods but stays within the auspices of Agreement. Nonconformists still find hope and value in vote and prayer. They intend to gain a share in property and authority.

The human being who is negative in his thinking and critical in his analysis is capable of breaking all ties with entity. The thinking human being has no need of supplication, because he can invoke his own mind as will. Capable of creation beyond mental Impasse, such person has no need for symbols upgrade because he is a mover of symbols and progenitor of a Self-world that is not a part of the made real but that can exist beside it as parallel. The man who is capable of negative thought knows calm. Past the juncture of The R.I.P. that feeds burden with noun inversion and reversals, he is host to the magic and beauty of something that can be called life. Beyond doubt, the last reciprocal is matched. In the realm of the unreal, parallels join. Reason and feeling can be one in First Voice, pressed again to rudimental Self dignity.

For the human being who can feel to Reason, life has no meaning because it needs no meaning. This is calm. This is silence.

Without ersatz momentum and the thrust and turmoil of symbolic time, The Creature is alive—alive in a world that can be like a waking dream where all symbols are intact as real and never the made real.

If the human being is to survive as a specie, the mental gap between Reason and feeling must be joined. The consumption of Self cannot continue without the final replacement to The Creature, human. As a specie, we are running on empty. We must come to the place that all momentum in time will cease. Every Creature must find pause to take a look inside, below the painful tear of The R.I.P.—the place where feeling and Reason can dissolve to zero: place where the dream becomes the life.

We cannot afford the made-meant-mean entity of Paradox that has been used as the commerce of supply and demand for the past two thousand years. We have no supply: Reason is spent. The circle of Blame produces strife and conflict only. Empowerment of The Retrograde in Reason slick and certified jargon is empty accomplishment and vain hope—the glorification of symbols upgrade.

Symbols upgrade is the illusion of transference, by jargon, of inferences—the moving and exchange of noun and verb for purpose that does not serve. In future, we are becoming life antithesis. It is no more than lexical gymnastics and the trade of black for white, when neither have any bearing but false gain and loss, false value and act.

In symbols upgrade, sanctimony is for the memory of last Reason held and that is held in Impasse for shared virtue.

The R.I.P. is contingent upon the upgrading of motive and always new parasitic good that gives future motive its always-increasing Reason for Reason and jobs for jobs made fact.

Progress is justification of warrant. Time is signifier of Self-departure and future is personification of failure on the tilted pathways of the human being in R.I.P. The heart of man is pale and diminished in the bright flashes of temporal flare that is the quick change of the rightful tenets of Agreement.

To recognize R.I.P. is an insanity that is equal only to the promise that it could all possibly be worth it.

NOTES

NAME: DATE:

XXIII

────────XXIII────────

SEEKING ADVANTAGE

The Slavery of Success and the Final Failure

It is the greatest of advantages
to enjoy no advantage at all.

—Henry David Thoreau

SINCE EVERYONE IS DOING THE SAME THING, there is no advantage in a think-factory system of Agreement. However, hypothesis or supposition is used as advantage through manipulation of meaning or denoted meaning for word slick. This sort of manipulation of imagination and imagined symbols makes Reason for Blame and Reason for contention possible and lethal, when in partial fact, there is no Reason for anything except as made to mean.

Advantage is decoy for the continuation of progress. Its promise is temporary and capricious. Advantage is Reason for Agreement to fail. Advantage, despite its promise of gain, is the means by which we hide from ourselves precisely what we seek. Seeking advantage is method of disregard. It is distraction and it is filler.

Progress is the manifest effect of advantage, for progress is based on Agreement to seek advantage. This the deception of noun inversion. We have only to look around us to understand that the progress of The Retrograde is pillage. Improvement is impoverishment and ruin. Improvement is the advantage of cutting costs.

Under the guise of benefit, atrocities are condoned and

upheld by law. Curing of disease is unimportant. The relief of physical suffering is unimportant because advantage is the gauge by which is measured the extremes of who will live and who will not have advantage to live.

In latter-day R.I.P. there can be no altruistic society, though in mindspeak we will believe it so because we hear it in The Voice of It and we see it in Its accompanying pictures. In R.I.P., we are assured of our goodness by our power. What is good through power is enforced. Power to enforce is advantage.

In R.I.P., we are tilting toward an axis where advantage is the only good. We are approaching a point where if one does not possess advantage in The Word, one is adrift from basic needs and cut off. This does not mean that the most poor among us will suffer the most. The most poor among us have agencies of relief that are in place for provision of right word usage. The fact of their helplessness is capital gain more for the entity of sloth.

Others, who cannot afford advantage but who are considered too wealthy to be counted among the idle poor for strategic advantage, feel the strain of two classes—above and below them—seeking advantage. They feel it because advantage can no longer be earned with hard work and skill but is failsafed through number and contained within legally proscribed parameters of idiom in sub-parallel and sub-group. There is no advantage unless it is purchased by numbers.

Advantage is procured by group muscle and, in order to have advantage, the individual must, first, Agree to measurable disadvantage. Focused Blame must be applied. It is impossible for even those with utmost advantage to pay. In order to have advantage, one must pay a premium to group that sells and governs it for Intended disadvantage.

Highly skilled technicians, whose minds are valued for memory, have little say. Expertise is meaningless in terms of decision. Decisions are dictated by office clerks who have been trained in electronic voice and word process. Clerks—craftsmen of the word with certification—have authority over expertise. Experts decide nothing. Expertise is not other than highly compensated slavery, and it is slave to the dominion of the consecrated clerical. In advantageous disadvantage, low-level menials decide while the disadvantaged seeking advantage pay large sums for the disadvantage of protection: Our health is insured so that we may continue to pay. We must ask ourselves: What is the inverse of protection? How are we being used?

To solve a riddle, one must accrue knowledge of opposition. If love is hate and protection is impairment and group bravado is fear, what is the effect of these things? The effect is the altered state and altered state is a pillar of words.

We are caught inside a labyrinth of parallel meaning and reciprocal match that is alarming and bewildering. It is not the gadgets of our invention that enslave us but our willingness to comply to the machines that we have made us!

What is Retrograde but a drudge to future past? The human being has been reduced to nothing other than the fleshy hands of a clock. The human being is nothing other than its own icon in history. What is sold as life is worthless. Life, in R.I.P., is nothing but dull passage of time.

Seeking advantage in R.I.P. causes a domino effect that builds as Reasons are stacked for advantage. Reasons stacked are held in Impasse until ready for use in strategic advantage. When used, Reasons fall against each other and set off a progression of Reason for Reason that is used for advantage.

Advantage is manipulation of values for fixation in one stable position. It is the falseness of our illusion that agreed stability lends advantage. But what we name advantage is nothing more than the fortification of false promises.

Advantage is Agreement to sham and it fails. It fails when we attempt to utilize it for need; when we realize that what we have agreed will not protect us but will serve entity well. It will not protect us precisely because it is for advantage. To have need to use it implies disadvantage. As soon as we attempt to use our investments in agreed advantage to ward off disadvantage, we become disadvantaged. Labeled as disadvantaged, we can no longer possess advantage and we are cut off from it and cast out.

It is desirable to purchase and to own advantage, but it is not intended for use in adversity. Side effects of disadvantage are not permitted. Advantage is intended for group gain only, and it is for the gain of the few and the misuse of the many—for procurement of gain.

Advantage is false safety for the minions and true accretion for the sector belonging to the charge of censure for advantage. All advantage is part of the cycle of Blame.

Individuality is not prized. To be said to possess a mind of one's own is the same as being labeled cantankerous or eccentric or even diseased. Critical thought, in its flowing and temperate content, is near criminal. Those who ponder and introspect exist on a plane that defies belief and are called neurotic and eremitic. The misanthrope is anyone who dares to live alone in thought.

The subscription to duty for Reason is mental gluttony. Duty for Reason and for consummation of advantage for disadvantage is no more than filler in want of valor. The Retrograde is cowardly and gutless. He finds his only safety in numbers and his satisfaction in Agreement. The Retrograde must be filled with vainglorious Reason for constancy or he will not continue, and he will not continue unless he can see progression, for Progression validates and upgrades his oblique want for safety and group failsafed advantage. A problem occurs when Reason and progress begin to backslide even as Reason is heralded as paramount advantage.

This is the beginning to the age of Reason fantastic. The believer in Reason will believe anything as long as it is kept under the veil of Reason. He will believe as he has been taught to believe no matter the consequence. Retrograde will sacrifice anything for the sanctioning of his belief. In the end, he will sacrifice himself and he will sacrifice even his Reason, if necessary, for the idolatry of belief. For advantage, we will sacrifice anything in disregard of ourselves and the completeness of our lives in Now.

When the human being suffers most is when he is out of context with his own agile and dynamic mental processes. Out of touch with his own innate ability to think and to deduce, he becomes his own Self-burden. Trust comes from unadmitted fear. Group thought and factory-think, while seeming to placate human misery, actually compound and escalate it. Jobs for jobs and results for results do not soothe the human Beast but further bind him to frustration upon disregarded frustration. Living inside the faint borders of importances, the human being must invert. Otherwise he will choose to live outside Agreement and importances will diminish.

Hypocrisy has no importance to the disagreeable miscreant except that it is the last means of sucking the last ounce of substance from the living being and, once the passive mind has opened, he is wary of it. Within the importance of hypocrisy, the human being is his own victim. We deplete ourselves. It is easy for Retrograde to house himself in such an empty shell. He is Self-consuming. We are in business of annihilation.

We empty ourselves of substance in trade for advantage, and advantage is perfect deceit.

What could be the advantage of deceit? What could be the advantage of misery? They are for the advantage of the few against the many. Those who are most masterful of deception in word use because of higher education have advantage. The rest are at their mercy. Mercy is the meaning of the hunt.

When those of religion speak of "seeing the light," what light is it that they inadvertently speak of seeing? If it is the light of life that lies dormant inside us, then we can have no need of restitution, for we have been shown how to hide that light and we have been deceived into selling the light.

We do not have to be tutored and cajoled and penalized and scolded into seeing any light. We are born with the light that lives inside us. We came from perfect nothingness with no ulterior voice, with a fully tender and pacific voice, with capacity for the most perfect whole sense that is five to the fifth power consciousness. We can have no need to find what is there intact from birth—that has no price; that is the spark and the light of life.

The price of slavery on the human being is implanted from birth. Beauty is timeless and has no tariff.

The price of slavery upon the human being is heavy and it is completely warranted. Yet the thing inside us that is life can have no warranty and no guarantee. It is our sadness that we refuse.

Life without perfidy has no advantage. There are no slaves to celebration. The sadness of our lives is its certainty. Uncertainty is magnificent joy.

Dignity lives alone and knows the horrors placed in the human heart. Seeking advantage is the seeking of The R.I.P.

NOTES

NAME: DATE:

XXIV

———— XXIV ————

GUILT

Ultimate Godhead and the Empowerment to Proscribe

> Laws are like spider webs: If some poor, weak creature
> come up against them, it is caught; but a bigger one
> can break through and get away.
>
> —Solon

THE HUMAN BEING, AS RETROGRADE, is unworthy of anything that could be like guilt in feeling. Correct assessment assigns guilt in Reason. The noun, guilt, is used as artifice for exacting function. What could be described in feeling as profound remorse and shame are not to be found in this world because Retrograde is incapable of such feeling. Remorse and shame would demand change, and Retrograde is unwilling to change and is set upon his course of destruction.

If the slave was capable of remorse, he would not be slave.

Retrograde, the slave, is unfit for change because change would signify an end to indifference and complacency. Since the slave considers himself as also master, he is impervious to change, and he makes his mind impenetrable.

Guilt, then, is not feeling, but a witting application of Reason. Guilt is a staple ingredient for a beggar's banquet of the mind. As a device, it succors us with empty platitudes that are weaknesses and inane bromide.

Guilt, as an application, is taught to us. Schools are the largest distributors of subliminal guilt. Through the austerity and inflexibility of standards and expectations, schools force children into habit and control of habit, and this is most easily inflicted and governed by use of guilt machination. Goodness, in the form of complete Agreement and conformity to rules of quiet servitude, is rewarded with goodness that is forward of now intention.

Evil, in the form of boldness and original thought—a natural inclination to use one's own mind and talent is condemned. Schools do not impart knowledge nearly as much as they impart mechanized guilt. In grade school, a child does not study reading and math and science as much as he studies and belabors the function of guilt. A child does not gain wisdom but gains a false sense of either extreme worth or extreme worthlessness. When a child feels that he has value, he has successfully complied with the rules of Agreement in guilt, and he is made worthy of the Agreement Process.

A child who will not comply, or who by his inherent nature cannot comply, is worthless, and is made to believe himself less. Such a child has guilt pressed upon him by marks of implied failure or by a systematic network of labels that signify guilt. If a child has no obvious physical defect, a suitable defect will be found for him through diagnostic guidelines. In this way he is forced into Agreement, and it will not matter that he fits the Reasons that are made-meant-to-mean and that are enforced, because Reason dictates that he will fit such constrictions by any means possible. By any means possible means that it does not matter that the child may grow up to be a felon. Through guilt, criminality is encouraged: How is it that schools and prisons look the same from the outside? If a child grows up to be a thief, this is acceptable because he has gained place in Agreement. A prison cell is agreeable.

What is not agreeable is the human being who, through his own resourcefulness of mind and determination of will, is capable of critical thought. Mental resource and will are drugged and categorized and made obscure. The sound capability of individual thought is, by Agreement, the ultimate transgression against the imposition of Reason.

Children are heavily penalized for thought because they are taught not to think, but to process-think. If suddenly freed, children would destroy the civilized world because if anyone ever stopped to ask the children, they would say it: "We loathe our constrictions and we are weary of our ties." Left in the hands of children, there could be no world of Reason as contention or Blame. There could be no provision of mechanized guilt and there could be no adults who practiced guilt. Children would destroy them, and they could do it with laughter alone.

The mechanism of made guilt is designed to have an enemy. The enemy of guilt may be a rivalry for possession of love or may be one who possesses more material goods or one who does not possess enough material goods. Jealousy dictates guilt and guilt feeds from jealousy.

Sometimes mechanized guilt takes on the guise of rejection. Often someone will reject the touch of a human being because he has been taught, carefully, that touch is wrong. When one agrees to believe that touch is wrong or that touch is favor, one complies to the belief in guilt.

Duty aligns guilt. When one is satisfied with this arrangement or when one agrees with it and designates worth over sensitivity, he is in Agreement with guilt even when he speaks loudly against it. In this way he will designate a lower station for those who can touch him most emotionally. Duty, by guilt alignment, conquers all.

Destinies, through Agreement, are poisonous. All groups are potentially very dangerous. The Reasonable man, through guilt alignment, will gleefully, and in trust, destroy the very thing that he loves the most, and he will do so without hesitation, and without compunction, and without care for sadness. Duty is guilt by association. Guilt is group thought. No group can exist without Blame or reverence for the power of word labyrinth.

Synthetic guilt is manufactured through invention of truth. Truth is good, as sold by Reason. Without invention of truth, there could be no such things as good and evil. Truth is failsafe

to the cycle of Blame, and those who are blamed are the miscreants of truth. Those who refuse to sell half their life essence
over to Paradox in R.I.P. are guilty of disobedience and disbe-
lief and the denial of a system of truth that is Blame.

Silent guilt, in the passivity of feeling can be palpated down
to the bone of the being and is without contortion of false suffering. Man, The Retrograde, has no capacity for the mute feeling of guilt, for it surpasses his set bounds in Reason, and Retrograde is brittle—will not expand.

Is it still yet possible to imagine the guilt of the man who was
called Christ? His awareness was his death, and his death was
his will and desire. If it can be said that Christ failed, then he
failed in Reason. He never failed in emotion and resolve to tenderness. The guilt of Christ was not his burden but the burden
of others placed upon him to imbibe.

Christ had no need of proof because his life and death were
proof. If his living and his dying were proof, then guilt was in his
eye. In the turmoil of his mind, he saw the proof of guilt, and he
saw its stamp upon the living essence of the human being, and
he saw its mark. By its etching upon the human essence, he saw
Reason for suffering and he knew Reason for misery.

The man called Christ well knew the Reason for his death.
One who does not fabricate Reason for living will pay a penalty,
and the penalty is harsh. One who, by the strength and conviction of his will to life, will not comply with restrictions upon his
actions, will be penalized. One who, by the strength and the
conviction of his will to life, will not comply with set laws and
values that are set against his will to life, will pay serious penalty,
and the penalty is atonement. Either, like Christ, he will be
forced to forfeit his life completely and as example or he will
be coerced or intimidated into relinquishing control, portion
by portion, until nothing is left. Within the conscription of the
made value that we call life, we are already dead. If we are
already dead, then nothing can be lost.

This is what the man called Christ knew: Born into Reason,

we are dead at birth.

Life is defunct. The human being is outlawed. Feeling is misfit. The panoramic spectacle of life that could be at our fingertips has been reduced to a series of numbers that add up to
nothing. The only truth is the glorification of the lie. Our lives
are for existence only—and the privilege of deceit.

If there could be something like bitterness in the essence of
the human being, then it is time to let it show. Are we not
weary of being chattel? Are we not weary of our slavery to mastery? Can there be no Resolution of time? Have we the stomach
to allow our children, through disregard, to become The Retrograde—man without a face, without question, without mind?

Do we dare to teach our children the material of Christ or do
we teach them submission? If the man who was called Christ so
loved the lowest among us, do we teach our children moral hate?

Within the altered state that is the mind in Reason, we have
no capacity for guilt that is silently resolute and that is knowing
without the penalty of knowledge. The silence of guilt is inside
the realm of fear.

Synthetic guilt is implemented with intention to Blame within
a firm circle of Blame. The loop that is formed by group mind
in Blame is infinitely wide and reaching. It touches us all and it
changes what is profound feeling into emptiness.

We are content in profound hypocrisy. We have no doubt. We
Agree through the power of our vote and prayer and through
the intricacies of lexicon. The Word is final truth and we all
obey.

The human being, through natural deductive thought and
feeling, has access to a sea of life. It is our failure that in Agreement we do not choose it.

Things are not complex except as we select complexity.
Things are quite simple, for it boils down to the one question
of whether "to be or not to be." For too long, we have selected
"not being," and our Reasons have been sound and practical.

The end of Agreement is the end of time. The end of time is

the beginning of the human being in life. Zero is the finite space of Impassionment of the senses: Life without Reason and life without the closed mental windows of words; life that is not enslaved and contained; life that has not been bought and that has not been stolen.

The life of sensorial Impassionment can begin to imagine the guilt of Christ—the silent and imposed guilt upon a being of frailty and love.

N O T E S

NAME: DATE:

XXV

WORDS

Second Voice: The Subconscious Artifact

That a lie which is all a lie
may be met and fought with outright,
But a lie which is part of truth
is a harder matter to fight.

—Alfred, Lord Tennyson

No HUMAN BEING IS BORN WITH A WORD BASE INTACT. The Second Voice exists after the fact of a First Voice. It has been said that without words the human being has no recourse of communication; that without the use of words the human being is nothing and can have nothing.

In his beginning, the human being made up sounds that matched things that he saw. As he continued to name things, he saw that things became tangible and material and that if things were material, they could be owned. The root idea of noun was the rudimentary ordering of things in lineage and ownership. Secondary impressions formed beside feeling that was transited to deep emotional need. Secondary symbolic impulse became the marking of what is real for ownership. The written word became proof of ownership and the new, mechanical word could be manipulated and even deny itself in reciprocation of word importance.

The Word, in use for attainment, is the blessed will to ignorance of the human being.

Words are not necessary for observation or emotion or for giving and receiving affection, no matter the contention that may be wrought by them. The memory of words is separate from the human being. To remember and to say and to learn to repeat is not intelligence but is knowledge by rote processing of charged symbols for Paradox. Words are expressive of intention only and consigned to a sub-parallel of belief that is Impasse of the mind in Reason manifest.

The words that are used in this work are intended to dissolve, to breakdown to the moment that two minds pass in the stillness that remains.

Half Life is lived through word inhabitation: fear in lieu of Self resolved by fear. Words are the signifiers, not of the sensorial world, but of the split reality of form and function. Words, given charge, represent what the fully sensual Creature could not bear, could not sanction, could not justify with overbearing of the Self without being shattered and dislodged of sense. All words are pretended to exist as intent.

Alone, the human being could not need words to think. He thinks by subconscious artifact: Second Voice in First Voice sublimation. Beneath The R.I.P., the original Self can enjoy sensorial bathing of the Self in emotion—the fully dimensional silent and complete awareness of Self.

Word meaning is the injury of emotion. What is felt and seen in transited feeling has no meaning in the order of lawful lexicon. There is nothing in lexicon that can provoke or injure the human mind that is in resolve to feel into emotion—into First Language—that which cannot be substituted. Think-process cannot abide the world of feeling. It is filled only by emotional reserve.

This silent voice is known only when it snaps the Reasoned mind and lets it suffer to know and lets it adjust to realize. When the knowing of the inner voice is accomplished, the void of the passive mind is open again and able to expand. Memory is dispersed into feeling. Vision, in this realm, can be electrified. Sounds can be enhanced. There is no end to release unless even one word is uttered. As soon as words enter the world of explosive feeling that is creation, The Creature becomes uneasy. The human being in original voice is naturally quelled by duty to future. In his anxiety he is susceptible to the offerings of civilization—the profiteer—that gives placation to his ills. There is no redemption in escape through drugs, nor consuming liquids, nor false diagnosis, nor status, nor recompense—all offered at nominal fees.

Placation is the selling back of fear and the selling back of made moral good. Words are promised as exchange for obedience to reap the rewards of servitude.

Words are an artificial world placed over an already sensually intact and silent one. The noise of The R.I.P. suits us in our servitude, for we are distracted for profit and for consumption. Bondage starts with The Word that inverts and bends the essence of The Creature to the belief that distance is expressed in time, numerically added and subtracted in accountable Reason. Slavery is the justification as we are split and left afraid, as we are split and left undone. Without the false reward of Half Life in The R.I.P., benefit that could be done would be done for all. But all who benefit by Reason and Reason for Blame sanction it.

Blame forges its ready-made vehicle of fear which is authority. Fear in First Voice always holds question to make it fearful, while fear in Second Voice is the authority of law.

If knowledge were no longer a commodity for consumption, the human being could know without Reason to know, and he could know without authenticating. We could live without authenticated happiness that is the dictum of The Word. The living of life in present regard could be seen as quite bold and implacable. Re-made fear cannot be sold back to the human being in present regard that is resolve, and it cannot be sold because such a being has already known fear and made it his friend.

The eyes-behind-the-eyes resolve that stems from the introspection of the senses dissolves the made meaning of words in content and context and moving force. In resolve, salvation is unnecessary and hero is reduced. Now is the expedient of living voice in feeling.

The role of circumstantial good is played out in prettiness or that which is pleasing or determined pleasant in word. This accomplishes nothing for the essence of man except to turn him over to symbolic abatement and resignation to accept Paradox in Reason. The enticing sounds of pretty words are intended to induce surrender—the giving over of will to follow entity, the will of the entity of They. In groups, the will of the human being is lost. All groups are, in partial fact, very dangerous.

The sacrosanct Word becomes our endowment for redemption. But, in partial fact, words are the prying bars to open a Self that was once gloriously and wonderfully open but is now armored inside a cage of group option.

Words are suspicious. Until all words can be dissolved down into zero space, The Word is false. But as the senses, in resolve, open to service the human being in First Voice, the idea of God is present. The idea of God is present and the present is always confused as God Voice or divine revelation: desperation unto the end.

Zero space allows the being to see with nothing other than feeling. In feeling beyond words, The Creature can know stillness. But the very minute that The Creature moves, the senses cease to explore and they begin to record.

Word promise deceives us into altering the recording of our passive memory. Reason comes from a single fear that is not trembling but is the natural insight of The Creature after the moment of opening.

No single human being could circumvent this natural fear. It took the empowerment of group will. Group persuasion dictates why things happen the way that they do, for circumstances are molded by group motive with force.

Time is distance based on insistence for production that is consumption: Impasse to duty and loyalty to provocation and authority of truth obeyed.

The Word is the law, and it is enforced as law for institutional intention. All words must fit into altered state reality that is cut off from The Creature's wholeness of being. All words provide motive and verdict. All words exist in formula for noun that is form and verb that is function. All words are said to convey meaning and carry nothing more than effect that is based on agreed effect.

When the individual being is removed from this setting, it can recognize its Self-worth and its dignity.

All words convey worth that can only be accepted as worth if proved: No one can own land except in deed of word. The same applies to love, right, good and truth. These are artifacts that are symbols for exploit.

The Word: The Question

1. *Should words be trusted?*
   Only to the point that they are no longer needed.

2. *Do words hold meaning?*
   Not beyond the idea that one can obtain the likeness of what was in want of security. The meaning of The Word is possession.

3. *Can words define?*
   No. Word definition is by inversion and intent. Definition, by dual implication, is before the partial fact of Now.

4. *What are words?*
   Words are nothing other than secondary imprints on form and function that have been bought and sold. If they are not this, they exist only long enough to be absorbed by feeling. In this way, words are entertainment only.

5. *Do words come from or contain certain good or right or promise or God-promise?*
   Yes, and this is part of their inherent danger, for through inversion of good for betterment of the word in future, words hide murder and pillage and come to bear upon motive sanctioned by duty.

6. *Do words contain the personifications of our fears?*
Yes. All words warn and insist upon right to invert what
could be like the presence of God in the human being.
Order is enforced by its opposite.

7. *Can words hold virtue?*
No. Actions, not symbols, define the being. Virtue is a myth.

8. *Do words hold intention?*
In the ordering of justification, intention is the sequences of
words that are artifacts of old deeds in words made to fit a
Paradoxical context at Impasse for memory use, authorized
and warranted by agreed circumstance. This is called truth.

9. *Do ideas conclude meaning?*
Emphatically, no. All Agreement-processed artifact is before
the fact of Now. Outmoded word symbols are overlaid with
new variations. In word artifact, there are no ideas.

10. *Is a man ignorant without the command of words?*
Not ignorant, but incapacitated in symbols command to
order response to favored circumstance.

11. *Do words make one intelligent?*
Quite the opposite, and it is an opposite with conviction.
Authority makes inverted intelligence profitable.

12. *Are words powerful?*
No. Words are as potent as is the conviction or belief to
make them so.

13. *Is R.I.P. possible without words?*
No, at least not as Second Voice.

14. *Are words prejudiced?*
Yes, through proper nouns incorporated with the promise
of future past: inverted.

15. *Are words good or bad?*
Neither. Reciprocal ordering produces opposite effects.

Words that are Intended good will oppose good and words that are intended bad will oppose bad.

16. *Do words help mankind?*
Words are for control only.

17. *How do words affect our lives?*
Words manipulate us to act and react.

18. *Should we endeavor to stop The R.I.P.?*
Our freedom dictates allowance of master and slave.

19. *Is freedom slavery?*
Yes.

20. *Is slavery freedom?*
Yes. Both the concepts of slavery and freedom are word-subservient, based on Agreement.

21. *Do words hold freedom?*
Yes. Freedom that is empowered conditionally.

22. *Without words, are we free?*
No. Freedom is not a question for a being quite sensitive and caring.

23. *Do we learn with words?*
No. We remember with word symbols. Learning is sensorial.

24. *Does The R.I.P. condemn words?*
No, only the manner of their use.

25. *In R.I.P., how do we acknowledge those things provided by word empowerment and authority through the Agreement Process?*
All instruction by word for enhancement of memory is oriented to power and position.

26. *Can the human being survive without words combined in Reason?*
Yes. He did so uninterrupted for 190,000 years.

NOTES

NAME: DATE:

NOTES

NAME: DATE:

AXIOMS

INTRODUCTION TO AXIOMS

We are all simple and common actors, and when we are not—when the veil is thinly worn or when the actor's mask is sheared—we are sad. And when in the coldness of our minds we refuse to be sad, we are afraid, and our fear is gaunt. When we are most afraid and forsaken, we are the most common and lowly.

Acting seems to be in our blood. We are so saturated in pretense that the acting becomes us. We are the characters of our imaginations, and as methods of our pursuits, our characters are as common as they have always been common in legacy and chained artifact.

The human being, without the mask of an actor, is a relic of history, for he can no longer exist—for existence is his cage and his bind, and he is given over to something different—an element that is not human but is something else—that is hardened and brittle and fast becoming old, as all machines become quickly old and are replaced.

Within the actor's made real facade, being is the same as not being, and the being behind the face has no bearing except that he is prisoner of his own will—except that he is chattel of his imperfect design.

We are not common in our trespasses nor in our constructed wrongs, and we are uncommon in feeling when feeling is unmasked.

What is this thread that we have pulled until we fade completely, even from our own vision? What is this mystery that we long to unravel? What in this cold distance between place and time that, inside the riddle of the heart, we long to measure and define? What is the split between the common and uncommon? What is the reflected image of chasm into chasm? What is the certainty in the deluge of time?

If we could take and never look back, or look back and never have given, what could be the veiled Reason for our division? What is the Reason for our mask?

AXIOMS

1 Nonviolence is a false sacrifice to a false God, and violence is a sacrifice of real human beings to real reasons.

2 God is a very serious mystery, and like most mysteries, does not need solving.

3 Wholeness of being is unity of mind. The mind in hypocrisy is a mind divided.

4 A treasure is a full coffer while others are empty. Discontent is never more, but always less than equal.

5 Struggle has but one meaning, and that is the struggle to control meaning.

6 When we finally learn that there is no meaning, there will be no conflict in meaning.

7 There is no courage among men, nor should it be asked. We were born cravens and our cowardice is our right.

8 The human being is a gentle creature. Our anger is our submission.

9 To feel fully is to know that reason, if pursued diligently, will lead directly to the heart of all conflict and to the fear that proves it.

10 Strength is an ambiguous word used carelessly by fools who promote freedom as power.

11 All suffering is false suffering for acceptable reasons.

12 Suffering is token payment for token promise.

13 Promise is the reason for Agreement that suffering should exist.

14 Heaven is a lighted ceiling over one continuous day.

15 Vindication of right that is caused by wrong is more bloody than any wrong justified to enforce it.

16 All groups are dangerous.

17 Government is the instrument of the peoples' mindlessness, as is religion.

18 The nature of man can be called upon to exhibit either brutality or gentleness; that which is wanted for obedience is called forth by reason.

19 Freedom that is protected by containment is merely a containment for fear.

20 To banish anger all that one must do is to study the actions of an enemy and what is being said. The why of anger will be obvious. The reply to anger is question.

21 One cannot have faith in oneself as long as belief is required.

22 Flaws are not mistakes in our characters, but are, rather, mistakes in understanding.

23 A man with a gun, by his need of a gun, will kill when given the chance.

24 A want to kill is neither good nor evil, but is only the reason necessary to pull the trigger.

25 Feeling does not make bullets fly, but given reason, bullets will fly.

26 There can be no resolve in knowledge.

27 Once in the middle, freedom is overwhelming.

28 No god could ever create subjects who feared him. Only the false god of man could subject us in fear.

29 The making of history is the making of reason for history. When time stands still, man will be blessed with the stoppage of sin.

30 Reasons are necessary, but not to the order of making one feel, and are not designed to be controlled by exclusivity of law and doctrine.

31 Meaning in reason is without dimension and shape.

32 Humankind is prepubescent in mental discipline.

33 Faith is not one's ability to wait for the optimal effects of truth. Faith is the stopping of faith for where one must reside for the lack of it.

34 Life is perfect at all junctions except one.

35 Justice that controls is injustice.

36 Fiction comes closer to truth than fact, and fact is nearly always fiction.

37 Religion is the control of those who amass from fear.

38 Anger enforces a goal. The want for anger is also the excuse for the goal.

39 Art belongs to feeling most exclusively despite any snobbery.

40 The written word belongs to reason that is reason to define feeling.

41 Art is a victory of feeling.

42 Power is power because it is allowed.

43 Beware of belief. It is a blind trust in a thing not altogether decidedly human.

44 Giving up one's life for a cause may be easier than living it.

45 Morality is the selling of man's fear.

46 Commitment is man's excuse for reason.

47 Fear will neutralize all reason into a steady flow of unreasonable importance.

48 There is no greatness in man that is beyond some simple dignity.

49 A war of supremacy is a war of meaning over meaning.

50 Nonviolence is the place that existed before reason entered.

51 We are flesh and made from flesh. Reasons, beyond flesh, endure.

52 The failure of nonviolence is that for reason, we are violent.

53 Fear makes heroes of others.

54 Compromise is fatal to the bearer of it.

55 Marriage is the rapid twisting of affection for reason.

56 In the concept of God fear, something is amiss. What is amiss is a contradiction in terms.

57 Fear of fear makes misery salable.

58 If man is provoked, he can no longer be contained, and he is released from the memory of his prison: I have been provoked.

59 We can see ourselves only through the eyes of others, and even then, the view is flawed.

60 To think is to doubt, and to doubt is to know the root from which all thinking comes: Original feeling.

61 Democracy is based on fear and sold as fear.

62 There has been no working principle yet designed.

EPILOGUE

The R.I.P. is a calling forth of continuing question from which can come a clear look at what lies behind the frontage of the mental picture. The R.I.P. is not a picture puzzle to be assembled, but it is, rather, a puzzle from which pieces have been removed. The R.I.P. is the removal of the shroud that covers life—the removal of the grim mask which is our excuse for life.

There are no meanings meant that can tell the whole of it. Convenient dualistic think-process terms, labels and symbols do not suffice to tell it. The story of The R.I.P., by will to Self-feeling, is outside the brotherhood of assent that declares, "We Agree to make it so."

The R.I.P. is like the scroll that expunges itself even as it is unrolled. The essence to it is silent. It is the one brief moment in which you can be sure.

Redoubtable, then, in calm, and stalwart like a bird in thin air, the story of The R.I.P. is timeless as some people are timeless and some things.

James Philip Beyor

SUPPLEMENT

The R.I.P. is about inductive word use as it applies to use by Agreement. Only by inductive commitment do words obtain authority to become implication of Intent for meaning. Words for Intent preclude entirely the possibility of deductive, critical thought. Deductive thought is labeled negative and therefore undesirable.

Deduction pulls down word premise into a variety of Reasons for cause and effect that remain intact. Words are a poor representation of want and desire. Intent is confused with emotion as the senses scrape the shell of intent away to reveal what is like a seed or a bone; the pith of the human being; substance; the essence.

Essence is the concern of man. The mind of man cannot assess all information held in passive memory—that which belongs to five separate compartments that are the five working senses. Each sense relates exactingly to its partner senses, but when one sense is given more importance than the others, an imbalance occurs that can increase nervousness and anxiety and fatigue. When, by noun use in Reason, the senses cannot reason with feeling produced from things that are inverted and reflected in the mind, a suffering occurs, and such suffering is the opening to Now—the eminence of Sixth Sense.

Fear cannot exist in a creature unless the senses have been skewed. They are skewed when one sense is more active than the others. Fear can increase proportionately to the speedy disregard of feeling. We were not designed to live for memory or from memory of symbols ensnared in memory.

This is where The R.I.P. enters and fear of fear becomes emblematic terror. In R.I.P., man has found a remedy, not a cure. The remedy is that, if everyone could agree to agree with that which has been made to mean, relief from fear could be found in words, and word relief could free man to conduct business as usual.

But the scam cannot work, not even in total and unrestricted Paradox of Reason.

Reciprocation in Paradox is the human condition. It is the human condition that can bear no lie but is the lie. It is the human condition that teaches good while abiding what is denoted bad until it is considered good. It is the human condition based on the imagination of ersatz momentum: the imagination of an altered state imposed on the frail back of The Creature that is human. We do not care, but we pretend to care because there is profit in pretense. We do not care but we exercise caring as a guise: How can caring be the turning away of things, and how can caring be the formulating of Reason that is the justification for hatred in caring? How can we care enough to maim and deform? How can we care enough to obliterate and destroy? How can we live in a world of refuse and care? How can we claim to care when our caring is murderous?

We purposely select ignorance as our master. We purposefully select Blame. The will to ignorance is our forsaking of all that is not knowledge. With knowledge, we long for the ultimate failure, for failure is The R.I.P.

The Impassioned creature knows this.

DERIVATIVE
RE-CONVERSION TABLES

Past—illusion of forward

Present—illusion of by-product effecting *en masse*

Future—illusion of rearward

Time—transpiration

Ego—reason command *en masse*

Consciousness—sensorial intuition

Subconscious—symbolic implant manifest

Sub-subconscious—sensorial interrogative based on zero divisible

Reality—R.I.P.

Fact—circumstantial paradox

Truth—circumstantial paradox impasse

Fiction—paradox

Lie—violation of circumstantial impasse

Good—agreement processed *en masse*

Bad—violation of agreed duty

Right—justification systems control

Wrong—violation of justification warrant

Feeling—circumstantial reactionary impetus

Emotion—overall reactionary impetus

Doubt—deductive question

Thought—question

Thinking—inductive premise

God—symbolic authority over natural fear

Evil—symbolic authority over all fear

Genius—symbolic premise granted and revered

Invention—assembly

Creation—tampering

Love—possession

Hate—want to possess

Guilt—nondevotion to duty

Sin—duty

Law—justification protection

Agreement—mutual benefit conscription

Belief—following

Fear—single sense cut off from sensorial whole

Reason—justification

Sense—physical interrogative to whole

Sensorial—physical interrogative of whole

Passion—mono-sense extreme

Impassionment—dimensional access; reason to feel

Blame—reason justification

Blame Loop—reason justification system

Impasse—last reason held for agreement

Paradox—last reason failsafed by agreement

Apocalypse—inevitable strife by reason

Word Labyrinth—inductive symbolic proprietorship

Joy—lasting unity of consciousness and subconscious

Happiness—temporary unity of reason

Knowledge—inductive premise

Wisdom—inductive premise deduced

War—power to reasons applied

Affection—uninhibited resource

Concern—unconditional attention

Dignity—self awareness

Progress—R.I.P. transpiration

Words—contrivances

Meaning—contrivance verification

Definition—differentiation

Wholeness—sensorial readiness

Purpose—configuration

Moral—duty glorification

Ethics—duty intensified

Intent—made want

Need—impulse

Noun—status to or for impetus

Verb—momentum to or for impetus

Care—concern uninhibited

Perfection—nature

Connotation—*en masse* circumstantial sentiment

Denotation—*en masse* authorized conscription

Education—symbolic indoctrination

Learning—mental expansion

Sexuality—biological yearning

Entity—resultant end belief (intent vehicle)

I—prior to We ordination

We—prior to They ordination

They—failsafe to blame

Why—post illusional justification

Failsafe—reason for ignorance

Ignorance—power

Power—failsafe of ignorance

Slavery—will

Freedom—slavery

Half Life—life that is not life

Life—self awareness

BIBLIOGRAPHY

Recommended reading

* Allport, Gordon, *The Nature of Prejudice,* Addison-Wesley, 1979.

* Allison, Fitzsimmons, *Guilt, Anger and God: The Patterns of Our Discontent,* Morehouse Publications, 1988.

Ansbacher, Heinz and Rowena, *Individual Psychology of Alfred Adler: A Systematic Presentation in Selections from His Writings,* Harp C, 1964.

* Aristotle, *Niomachean Ethics,* translated by Martin Ostwald, Library of Liberal Arts.

* Bergson, Henri, *Creative Evolution,* translated by Arthur Mitchell.

Bharati, Agehananda, *The Tacit Tradition.*

Broad, Charles, *Ethics and the History of Philosophy: Selected Essays,* Hyperion, 1986.

* Campbell, J., *The Masks of God: Oriental Mythology,* Viking Press, 1962.

Corvin, *Plaintiff's Proof of Prima Facie Case.*

Dellamora, Richard, *Postmodern Apocalypse,* University of Pennsylvania Press.

* Facione, Peter, *Ethics and Society,* 2nd Edition, Prentice Hall, 1991.

* Fagothey, Austin, *Right and Reason: Ethics in Theory and Practice.*

Foucault, Michel, *The Archeology of Knowledge,* translated by Sheridan Smith.

* Freud, Sigmund, *Future of an Illusion,* Norton, 1984.

Freud, Sigmund, *The Mind of the Moralist,* 3rd Edition, Philip Rief, University of Chicago Press, 1979.

* Fromm, Erich, *Dogma of Christ: And Other Essays on Religion, Psychology and Culture,* H. Holt and Company, 1992.

* Gebser, Jean, *Structures of Consciousness,* Georg Feustein.

Goffman, Erving, *Interaction Ritual: Essays in Face to Face Behavior,* Pantheon, 1982.

Goffman, Erving, *The Presentation of Self in Everyday Life,* Doubleday, 1959.

Hall, Edward, *Hidden Dimensions,* Peter Smith, 1992.

Hardin, Craig, *Shakespeare: A Critical Study.*

* *Hegel's Idealism: The Satisfaction of Self Conscience,* edited by Robert S. Pippin, Cambridge University Press, 1989.

Hegel's Phenomenology of Spirit, Martin Heidegger, translated by Parvis Emad and Kenneth Maley, Indiana University Press, 1988.

* *Hegel's Philosophy of Right, with Marx's Commentary,* Howard P. Kainz, Kluwer, 1974.

Herberg, Will, *Protestant, Catholic, Jew: An Essay in American Religious Sociology,* University of Chicago Press, 1983.

Horwich, Paul, *Theories of Truth,* Dartmouth, 1994.

* Jung, C.G., *Psyche and Symbol: A Selection of Writings,* translated by R. F. Hull, Princeton University Press, 1990.

* Kant, Immanuel, *Collection of Critical Essays,* edited by Robert Paul Wolf.

* Kant, Immanuel, *Critique of Pure Reason,* edited by Ralph C. Walker, Ohio University Press, 1982.

Kant, Immanuel, *Kant's Life and Thought,* Ernest Cassirer, translated by James Haden, Yale University Press, 1982.

Kant, Immanuel, *Kant's Respect and Injustice: The Limits of Liberal Moral Theory,* Victor Siedler, Routledge, 1986.

* Kirkham, Richard L., *Theories of Truth,* Bradford Books, 1995.

Krimermann, Leonard and Parry, Lewis, *Patterns of Anarchy: Collected Writings on Anarchist Tradition.*

McClendon, James W., *Ethics of Systematic Theology,* Abingdon, 1988.

* Males, B., *The Philosophy of Liebniz,* Oxford Press, 1986.

* *Nietzsche,* Martin Heidegger, Vol. 1 and 2 / Vol. 3 and 4, translated by David Ferrell Krell, Harper Collins.

* Nieztsche, Frederick, *Ecce Homo,* translated by R. J. Hollingdale.

* Nietzsche, Frederick, *The Birth of Tragedy and The Genealogy of Morals,* translated by Francis Golffing.

* O'Neill, Reginald F., *Theories of Knowledge,* Irvington, 1980.

Rand, Ayn, *The Fountainhead.*

Rand, Ayn, *We, The Living.*

* Rand, Ayn, *Capitalism.*

* Rand, Ayn, *For the Intellectual.*

* Rand, Ayn, *The Virtue of Selfishness.*

Rand, Ayn, *The Romantic Manifesto.*

Rand, Ayn, *Early Ayn Rand.*

Roscoe, Gerald, *The Good Life: A Guide to Buddhism for the Westerner.*

Roznak, Theodore Roznak, *The Making of a Counter Culture: Reflections on the Technocratic Society & Its Youthful Opposition,* Upclose Publications, 1995.

Rudnytsky, Peter and Spitz, Ellen, *Freud and Forbidden Knowledge,* New York University Press, 1995.

* Ryle, *Critical Essays,* edited by Oscar Wood and George Pitcher.

Sommerville, John and Santoni, Ronald, *Social and Political Philosophy: From Plato to Ghandi.*

* Stern, Rapheal, *Theories of the Unconscious and Theories of the Self,* Books Demand.

* Stringfellow, William, *The People Is My Enemy,* Concerned Publications.

* Swartz, Robert J., *Perceiving, Sensing and Knowing: Readings from Twentieth Century Sources on the Philosophy of Perception.*

Senzaki and Paul, *Zen Flesh—Zen Bones: A Collection of Zen and Pre-Zen Writings,* C.E. Tuttle.

Stryk and Takash, *Zen: Poems, Prayers, Sermons, Anecdotes, Interviews,* 1982, Swallow.

* Taylor, A.E., *Socrates: The Man and His Thoughts.*

Vlastos, Gregory, *The Philosophy of Socrates.*

Wittgenstein, *Mind and Language,* (Vol. 245), edited by Rosaria Egidi, Kluwer AC.

Wittgenstein, *Mind and Will, Volume Four of an Analytical Commentary on the Philosophical Investigation,* P.M. Hacker, Blackwell Publication, 1986.

REFERENCES

The Bible, King James Version.

West, Henry, *Black's Law Dictionary,* Fourth Edition Revised

INDEX

CT-LINK™

CT-LINK means Ceno Think or New Think. How man is willing to think affects what he thinks, and what he thinks is affected by how he must think. What is held in memory, for the purpose of resultant end, will always show up as existing intention. Process group-think is living thought inverted and justifies agreement to produce reason for reason and jobs for jobs entitlement and power.

> *CT-LINK™* is a newsletter for people who have read *The R.I.P.* If you seek deeper understanding of its ideas and wish to share yours, write for your free newsletter—your way to reach people from all over the world.

> *CT-LINK™* Letters seek responsible charge of personal freedoms which have nothing to do with expenditure of capital for promotion of human misery through deception.

> *CT-LINK™* seeks to restore, by the linkage of thinking, feeling people, what was once, through reason deduced by emotion, the essence of learning that is the center of life.

> *CT-LINK™* is about the individual first and about those individuals who may be loosely connected by their parallel needs of deep thought and emotion.

There is an inherent danger in our antiquated think-processing that can produce a specie that can capitalize on misery and legal provocation.

Please share with us your serious regard, your insights and aspirations. The mental door is sealed shut by reason and can only be re-opened with sincere self-feeling and expressed ardor.

For your free subscription, write to:

CT-Link
P.O. Box 1070
Buchanan, VA 24066

PRINTS

Beautiful Studio Quality Prints
with large, white border—
ready for 11 x 14" frame

Choose from seven bold prints
(also pictured in *The R.I.P.*).

III   VI   VIII   IX   XI   XVIII   XIII

$**9**^{95}_{EA.}$
plus $2.50 shipping & handling

Order two to six prints for $8.95 each
plus $3.50 shipping to one address —
OR order all seven for $59.50
and we'll pay shipping and handling!

Send check or money order to

C-T Prints
P.O. Box 1070
Buchanan, VA 24066

Be sure to indicate which prints you want
and include your return address!

Make a statement in life —
it all starts at home!

ORDER FORM

Additional copies of The R.I.P.

$**19**$⁹⁵

plus $3.50 shipping & handling
Order two copies for $36.95 + $3.95 S & H and save.

Use our toll-free number:

1-800-266-5564
HAVE CREDIT CARD READY

or order by mail:

Send check or money order to
The R.I.P. — C-T Publications
P.O. Box 1070
Buchanan, VA 24066

Please print your name and return address clearly.

Special One-time Offer—
While They Last

A signed hardcover Collector's Edition
with slipcase and dust jacket,
embossed in silver-color foil on exquisite linen.
Only 100 produced in first edition.

$**49**⁹⁵

plus $4.50 shipping and handling

Please state "Collector's Edition" when ordering.